The Consocratic Plan

A PLAN FOR THE PLANET

BY

TED WELLS

Cover and title page font: Toulouse-Lautrec
Text fonts: Book Antigua, Arial, Arial Narrow, Times New
Roman, Handwriting font: MICHAEL
Cover is a photograph of a 2005 village meeting in Siumu,
Samoa by the Author. All other photos, diagrams and
charts are by the Author.

ISBNs: 978-0-473-64100-9 (Softcover POD)
978-0-473-64101-6 (Kindle)
978-0-473-64102-3 (PDF)

TO
MY MUCH LOVED SONS,
TAO MCLAREN WELLS
AND IAN CRESSY WELLS

FOR THEIR UNSHAKEABLE BELIEF
IN THE POSSIBILITY
OF A BETTER WORLD
FOR US ALL

Acknowledgements

I would like to thank my wife, Helen Ann McLaren Wells, whose love, humor, intelligence and inspiration as my life's traveling companion for nearly 60 years has allowed me the time and space to put my ideas down on paper. I'd also like to thank my son, Tao McLaren Wells, whose creative thinking helped shape many of the ideas in this book, particularly those about the social blindness of capitalism and the many injustices inherent in our public institutions. Equally importantly, I'd like to thank my late son, Dr. Ian Cressy Wells, who showed me that life is not about the accumulation of wealth. It is about exploring, discovering and enjoying every day with family and friends.

There are many, many others who helped me clarify my thinking over the years. Some I've only known remotely through their work. Noam Chomsky has perhaps been the most influential, but there is also John Buck, the man who brought Sociocracy to the English speaking world. Others include Sharon Villines, Ted Rau, John Reuwer, John Rohrbaugh and John Schinnerer who continue John Buck's work, and Edwin John who independently developed a very similar system of governance across many parts of India.

I am indebted to all of you and to everyone else I've met on my life's journey. You have been my good fortune.

In peace and with thanks

TED WELLS

NOTE: This booklet is an excerpt (Chapters 19 & 20) from the Author's book "Power, Chaos or Consensus? How to Fix Our Global Melt-Down: A PLAN FOR THE PLANET". This larger book explains how the following plan was developed. For a chapter by chapter synopsis of the book please turn to page 137.

The Consocratic Plan

Table of Contents

Economic Rights and Responsibilities

Equity Rights and Responsibilities

Community Rights and Responsibilities

Environmental Rights and Responsibilities

Part 5: Fundamental Rules 53

INTRODUCTION
A Way Out of this Mess

Three things seemed clear to me back in 1972 when I first realised that most of our democratic institutions contained several serious flaws in them. One was that any attempt to fix them would need to take into account the intense, complex, ever changing chaos that we all have to live with on this planet. There is no reason to think that new life-changing ideas, inventions and problems would not continue to emerge as we all go through indefinable time.

However, chaos is not as random as the name implies. Mathematicians and other experts on the subject have shown that over time, discernable, often repetitive, patterns will eventually appear in chaotic events. The significance of any chaos is formed at its very beginning. If any pattern is generated by chaos, that pattern is actually set by the very first steps that occur seemingly randomly.

The Consocratic Plan contained in this book has focused on setting up that beginning event for precisely this reason. Even with a clear set of goals, principles, rights, responsibilities and rules, that is, with a much more detailed constitution, the ultimate form of any democratic government that considers the rights and needs of everyone on an equal basis in a sustainable environment and well functioning market economy will be almost impossible to predict.

The second thing that has been clear to me from the beginning is that the tools that our governments use to handle the chaos must, by necessity, end up as fractals; that is, be in a form that looks and acts the same way on many different levels of government. Public understanding of how governments work is absolutely essential if people are to support and participate in them.

The third is that any serious update of an existing democratic government must be introduced through the efforts of many small groups of people rather than through the efforts of either just one person or an entire country.

I had thought that change from either the top or bottom almost always required force, and one critical prerequisite I had

1

set myself from the very beginning was that a democratic solution to the planet's existing problems could not be achieved through violence, terrorism or war.

I have since discovered, thankfully, that my third concern may not have been entirely warranted. The very nature of consensus decision-making seems to generate peace and social tolerance among people rather than violence, terrorism or war.

Nevertheless, I have set out the following suggestions on how to fix the mess we're in on this planet by beginning with what small groups of people might do to start the process. Even if a Consocracy is established by one of the other two methods, the final step in all three approaches would be the same.

§

I know the likelihood of any government updating its laws to use consensus is extremely remote. If there was a quick fix to the problems we face we'd have found it by now. Certainly the five hundred sixty individually approached publishers and agents who "passed" on this book did not believe in the possibility despite specifically professing to have an interest in Political Science. Not even one bothered to read the full manuscript.

Their reluctance, I suspect, was at least partly because consensus decision-making is now a lost art among most communities on this planet. Even the best democracies today resolve problems by identifying two (or more) solutions and then forcing voters or their representatives to choose just one of them.

This unavoidably forces everyone to take sides. The process splits communities and creates winners and losers, which is often followed by a feeling of alienation and anger among those who lose out.

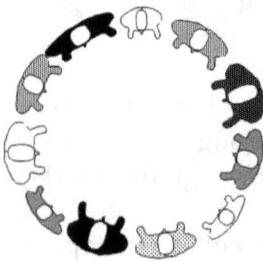

Decisions by Consensus   Decisions by the Majority

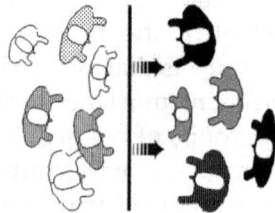

2

It is for this reason I believe that the single most important 1st step any of us might take to update our democracies and our chances of survival on this planet is to try to convince the people we live with, the people we work with, the people in any existing local group we are involved in to "Think Globally, Act Locally;" that is, to make their decisions by the consensus of everyone in that group rather than by a vote of the majority.

Examples:
- A family deciding where to go on vacation,
- Teenagers choosing the location of their next social gathering,
- A neighborhood group setting the theme for their annual street party,
- A sports club committee deciding who should be their next president,
- A community service club deciding what project to support,
- A town centre Chamber of Commerce setting the year's business support program,
- A university political science class deciding with their teacher what they will focus their studies on.
- A local government town planning committee deciding what developments to approve.

The motivation for a group to change its method of decision-making might be the noble desire of members to end paternalism and give everyone in the group equal power to make decisions. It might be the desire to bring a divided group, club or committee back together, or it might simply be the gentle push of someone who believes in the idea. In any event, the experiment would not require the group to change anything else.

Group, club or committee members would still be elected, appointed or volunteer as previously. No existing laws would need to change. Nothing would have to change other than that all group members would have to agree to talk through their differences and reach decisions without opposition. Remember, as used by "primitive" societies, consensus does not mean 100% agreement. It means there is no disagreement. The difference may sound like meaningless semantics but it is extremely significant. It means that all anger, hate and divisiveness have been removed from the outcome.

While reaching consensus in a group, club or committee might seem an improbable first step, there are actually a number of groups, committees, and even a few governments around this planet already leading the way. For instance almost all indigenous communities in the South Pacific make their local decisions by consensus. In addition, the British Guernsey Islands off the coast of France are now largely run by a series of committees that use consensus.

There are also two Canadian districts, the Northwest Territories and Nunavut Province that reach their decisions in part by consensus. More relevant to larger communities and governments, most of the 100 or so "Green" or environmental political parties around the world, many of which now have elected representatives in government, have used consensus to set their policies since the 1980s, and as pointed out earlier, most jury trials and Quaker meetings have used consensus decision-making for centuries.

To ensure some likelihood of success in replacing majority vote decision-making with consensus decision-making, any group or committee attempting to use consensus will probably need to be very small initially. It is much easier to understand the views of 10 or 15 people in depth than it is to get to know intimately the hopes and desires of 50 people.

Reaching consensus in small groups is not impossible, for even today most democracies do it every time they vote on anything. This may sound surprising, but every time a decision is made by majority vote, everyone on the majority side must reach consensus among themselves on the details of what they are actually voting to support. In a city council with 11 members, for instance, at least 6 members must reach mutual agreement on exactly what they are choosing to do. While there is likely to be less diversity of thought in half a group, some diversity, even among the majority half is usually unavoidable. So in reality, even majority vote decision-making often requires reaching consensus among a group of people.

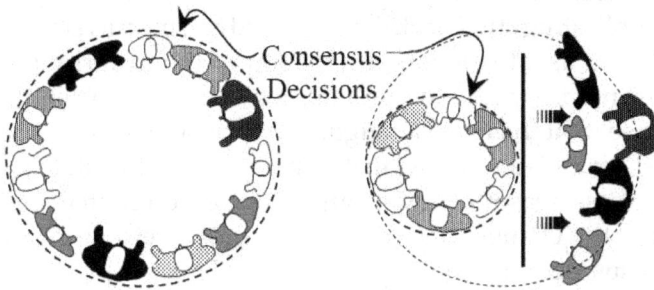

Decisions by Consensus   Decisions by the Majority

While most groups of people on the majority side don't actually vote among themselves when they decide what they will support in a full democratic vote, some do. In such circumstances, it means that only a majority of the majority, or as little as 26% of the people in that democracy are actually making decisions for the public. It means that the "majority" of people are not really running that government at all, not by any stretch of the imagination.

Just the change to consensus decision-making by a club or committee would create a fundamental shift in the group's approach to problem solving. Everyone knows how our current democratic decision-making works. In parts of the world it has been practiced for centuries. An idea is raised, its good and bad points are debated, and then it is voted upon. If more than half agree with it, the idea becomes applicable to everyone.

Unfortunately, today almost no one knows how consensus works. Most people only know that it's impossible to use in large groups and it can be hijacked by narcissists. In most of the world, knowledge of the art, value and practice of consensus decision-making has been lost for generations. In our modern world, few have ever had the chance to discover that decisions made by consensus are usually more holistic than majority vote decisions; that they unite communities rather than divide them; and that they are often cheaper and quicker to implement in the long run because they can be carried out immediately without the ongoing hassle of opponents trying to change the decision or stop its implementation.

Complicating this lack of knowledge, in current political debate the usual reaction of a person in the majority group to an idea not in sympathy with one's own, is to rubbish it. It is a response that has been taught over centuries of democratic contest, and it is a response that some will find difficult to give up.

For these reasons, any group, club or committee that does decide to change its majority vote decision-making to consensus decision-making will probably need to adopt some initial informal rules of conduct to help all members stay focused on the committee or group's usual tasks.

In most committees today, for instance, the chairperson's primary role is to keep order and ensure democratic processes are followed. In many committees, he or she does not even vote unless there is a tie and a "casting vote" is required.

A slightly revised role for the chairperson in a group using consensus might be for the chairperson to act as a neutral mediator to reduce tensions in heated debates, similar to the way a Samoan Orator manages a community meeting. The chairperson could also be the facilitator in identifying similarities between different ideas in search of a solution acceptable to all.

The chairperson might even be the person who is given responsibility for deciding what to do if consensus cannot be reached. For instance, he or she might be given by the others in the group, the power to invoke a previously agreed alternative means of decision-making in such circumstances, such as "consensus, less one".

In a fully operating Consocracy, there are better options when this happens, but in the early stages of setting one up, when consensus cannot be reached, a back up plan for the group's decision-making is a very good idea.

§

The reason why decisions will take more time in the early stages of consensus decisions-making, is because every member of a group must get to know intimately every other member of the group. It is not enough just to know every member's name. Each member must become sufficiently familiar with everyone else in the group to know their families, where they live, what their hobbies are and why they want to be a representative.

In a fully functioning Consocracy, it is a fundamental requirement that every group's representative must provide such information in writing and keep it up to date as part of the representative's public record.

Getting to know the other members in a group well can be shortened with the help of computers and the internet. Facebook, Twitter, Skype, WhatSapp, Zoom, FaceTime and other social networking tools used outside formal gatherings of the group are powerful methods of communication that can rapidly speed up understanding between people. Other computer aids worth considering include programs like BrainStorm, Loomio and Weaver, which facilitate the exchange of ideas, assist in problem structuring, and support decision-making processes.

Possibly the most powerful way that computers can help very diverse groups of people find mutually agreeable solutions to complex problems, however, is to use them to identify what a mutually agreeable consensus decision might look like. Dr. John Rohrbaugh's "Value Knowledge Management" computer program discussed earlier, for instance, can help such groups reach consensus by considering the values and interests of each person involved individually. By using a computer, group members can then begin their discussions from a known possible solution rather than try to blindly create one from scratch. This considerably improves the chances of a successful outcome.

§

I believe the successful use of consensus by a number of small local groups, clubs or committees will, in time, encourage local governments to try it too, and that would be a very significant 2nd step in introducing it to central or national government decision-making. This is because local governments have the legal right to affect the lives of many people through the powers they enjoy.

What they can legally make decisions on, of course, varies from community to community and from country to country depending on existing empowering legislation, but in most cases the governments of towns and cities can regulate private land use as well as collect taxes to pay for local public improvements like roads, parks, libraries, water supply, sewage treatment and other public services and facilities. Both are very powerful local democratic decision-making functions.

Like the 1st step, this would not require any changes to existing laws. I have not found any democratic government anywhere whose constitution prohibits its representatives from making their decisions by consensus.

All members of a local council would still have to be elected by the public in their usual way, but at that point they could then voluntarily agree among themselves to use consensus to make their council decisions. Using consensus would instantly change the outlook and image of a local government to the people it governed. This 2nd step in the adoption of a consensus based central or national government would inspire public cooperation and community spirit and it would encourage other communities to follow their example.

§

The 3rd step in setting up a consensus based national government would be to set up a method for local residents to become voluntary community advisors to local government to provide elected members with detailed knowledge of local activities. This too, would not require any law change.

Today, most local governments include not only elected representatives but non-elected advisors to help representatives make their decisions and to carry out the decisions local governments make. The advisors typically include experts like administrators, engineers, economists and planners, but there is usually no formal criteria or procedure that local governments must follow to select them, so some could be selected as "community advisors" by using a simple, informal version of "structured consensus decision-making". As described elsewhere, this is a multi-level method of choosing representatives by consensus.

The reason why this would be helpful is that most local governments have grown so large that elected representatives rarely know much about the inner workings of most neighborhood residential, commercial or industrial areas they represent or the lives of the people in them. Similarly, few local residents today have any understanding of what local governments actually do, much less how or why. The introduction of voluntary community advisors to councils would greatly reduce such ignorance.

At this early stage the use of structured consensus decision-making methodology to select the community advisers would not have to consider all the matters a full consensus based government or Consocracy might consider, but such a multi-leveled method for selecting them would encourage local residents throughout the jurisdiction of the local government to support and peacefully work together with their political leaders. The advisor positions and method of choosing them could be entirely voluntary and need not cost the local government anything.

The population of the area being governed would determine the number of "levels" needed for its volunteer community advisors. An urban/rural area with under 50,000 people might need only two or three levels of community advisors. If there were a million people involved, there might need to be four or five levels.

Once it becomes clear that "structured consensus decision-making" works to introduce community advisors into local government decision-making, it might then be possible to take the 4th step by widening the role of the volunteer local multi-leveled community advisors into other decision-making groups operating within the local government's jurisdiction. Initially, the most logical "community advisor" responsibilities might involve only land use management matters like helping council members decide the location of new housing or commercial buildings. However, the local parent-teachers group or school board in a town might consider it helpful to develop a close relationship with a local community advisor too since he or she would probably be involved in helping local governments determine where schools are built and how they might be expanded.

In time, other levels of government involved in public education, roading, health care, public utilities and community services might find it helpful and economically beneficial to add the council's voluntary community advisors to their own meetings to help them coordinate their activities. Such cooperation would help regional hospitals work with regional transport systems and higher education providers to ensure their accessibility to all those who need to use or staff them.

This is actually a more important part of the 4th step in the upgrade of a democratic government than it might seem, as the ultimate form of a Consocracy pulls together all forms of public decision-making into a single body at every level of government, and this 4th voluntary step would demonstrate how such a major change in political decision-making might work.

Under a fully operating Consocracy, local governments on each level would not only administer land use, but oversee public education, public health, justice and police services as well, with the assistance of sub-committees focused on these areas. The political responsibilities at each level would be much more explicit than they are now and would depend on the size of the geographical area and number of people they represented, but all government decisions would then be able to be much more holistic than they are now, as each of their decisions would have to consider all 5 types of systems of change previously discussed at once, i.e. personal, economic, equity, community and environmental change.

Up to this point, no laws would have to change. Local government decision-making by consensus would be voluntary and the establishment of community advisors would not require any new legislation.

§

However, the final step, Step 5, would unavoidably require updating existing laws. This last step involves updating an existing democratic government's constitution using part or all of the components set out in the Consocratic Plan, the final (20th) Chapter of this book. This step would require a "leap of faith" in the Consocratic form of government, and would probably only work once the general pubic of a whole country had become familiar and comfortable with how well and peaceful consensus based decision-making worked after successfully following the first 4 steps.

Given the major law changes that would have to be made by a whole country taking the 5th step, small island nations like the Virgin Islands, the Cayman Islands, the Isle of Man, or Bermuda might seem the most likely candidates to make such a change. Unfortunately, however, most island nations are tax havens heavily reliant on handling the wealth of international corporations in secret. They could not easily afford to make, much less lead, such a change.

More likely, any major attempt to set up a structured consensus based central government would probably have to be led by a small country with more diversified interests. Some countries, such as The Netherlands, Denmark, Norway, Sweden, Switzerland, Australia and New Zealand already have a history of social reform that might facilitate the introduction of structured consensus decision-making.

The final step could be taken simply by formally adopting the full Consocratic Plan included in Chapter 20 as an adjunct or replacement to an existing nation's constitution, or in some cases like New Zealand's, as its first complete constitution.

The full Consocratic Plan essentially has 8 Parts, which are:

Part 1. Plan Commencement
Part 2. The 5 Principles of a Consensus Based
Democratic Government
Part 3. The 12 Goals of Humanity
Part 4. The Rights and Responsibilities of both
Individuals and Groups
a. Involving Personal Systems of change
b. Involving Economic Systems of change
c. Involving Equity Systems of change
d. Involving Community Systems of change
e. Involving Environmental Systems of change
Part 5. Fundamental Rules
Part 6. Recommended Rules
Part 7. Termination
Part 8. Interpretation of Key Words

The constitutional update would not have to happen all at

once. It could happen in several stages. For instance, under the rules in Part 5, it is essential to assign a globally unique identification number to every individual and to associate all individuals with a publicly recorded, globally unique "site".

Both might best occur prior to any constitutional update. It is possible that this requirement might be opposed by some human rights advocates despite the substantial increase in individual rights that adoption of the Consocratic Plan would allow. The more time that is given to help people understand why they should be given a globally unique identification number and be associated with a single site, the more likely everyone will accept their introduction.

Public discussion of some parts of the new constitution might actually best occur some time after most of the new constitution is adopted.. In particular, Part 6 involves suggested tax and monetary changes which are not essential to the operation of a Consocracy so could be added at a later date.

Also, a number of the Rights and Responsibilities included in Part 4, namely those "recommended" in standard arial type like this and those "possible" ones *in light italics like this*, are not essential to the operation of a Consocracy. These could also be left out initially until there was an opportunity for everyone to consider them in detail.

The four diagrams on the right illustrate how the first three levels of "Structured Consensus Decision-Making Groups are formed, starting with what constitutes a "Site", then what "Neighborhood","Village" and "Town" levels might look like.

The last diagram on the following page schematically shows the organizational similarity of the various levels of decision-making groups. Every black circle in the diagram is a decision-making group of representatives.

The size of the circle identifies the number of people (and number of sites) it represents; the larger the circle, the more people (and sites) represented. Each black circle or decision-making group is set out and operated in the same way as every other black circle or group. The large black circle in the middle of the diagram is simply a detailed look at one of the decision-making groups on level 3. All groups on all levels actually look and operate like this.

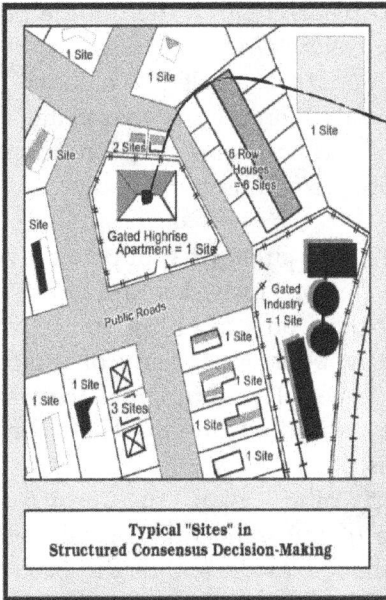

Typical "Sites" in
Structured Consensus Decision-Making

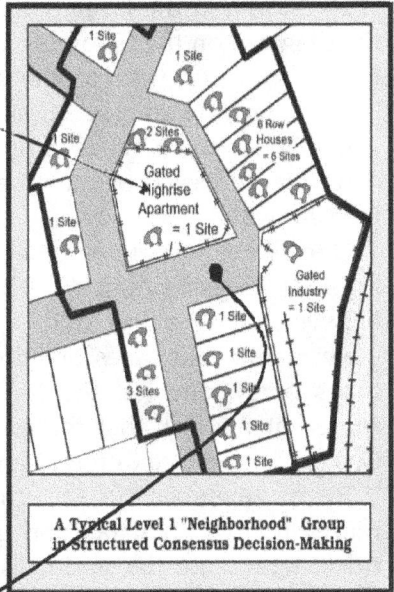

A Typical Level 1 "Neighborhood" Group
in Structured Consensus Decision-Making

A Typical Level 2 "Village" Group with
Representatives from 8 Neighborhood Groups

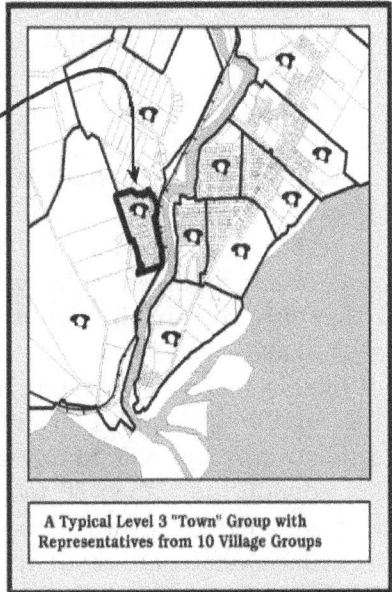

A Typical Level 3 "Town" Group with
Representatives from 10 Village Groups

As shown in the large detailed black circle in the middle of the diagram on the following page every circle or group is split into 6 sections. Five of the sections are labeled "Personal", "Economic", "Equity", "Community" and "Environmental", (PEECE) for the 5 types of systems each group decision must consider, and each of these sections contains two shaded and labeled ovals.

One of the 6 sections of each black circle or group is only labeled "Representative". This person provides the "link" between that group and a group on the next level of government, but takes no direct responsibly for any of the 5 types of systems on the lower level. The thin grey arrows represent the link that the same individual provides between two groups on two different levels.

Every member in a group other than the group's representative must take on one of the ministerial or cabinet roles, which are the variously shaded ovals within the black circles. For groups with less than 11 members some of these roles must be doubled up. For instance the member responsible for economic systems in a group with less than 11 members may have to take on both the Economist and the Lobbyist roles. For groups larger than 11 members, cabinet or ministerial roles should be shared.

What is most important is that at least one group member responsible for each of the 5 types of systems, as well as the representative linked to the upper level group must all be present and involved in every decision made by that group.

For this reason all groups must contain a minimum of 6 representatives, as shown by the 6 short arrows into the centre of the black circle which link the decisions of every member to the goals, principles, rights, responsibilities, rules and regulations applicable to that group. Preferably, groups should not contain more than 30 members so that all representatives may sit together in a single circle and easily talk with each other face to face, although up to 42 members are permissible in exceptional circumstances.

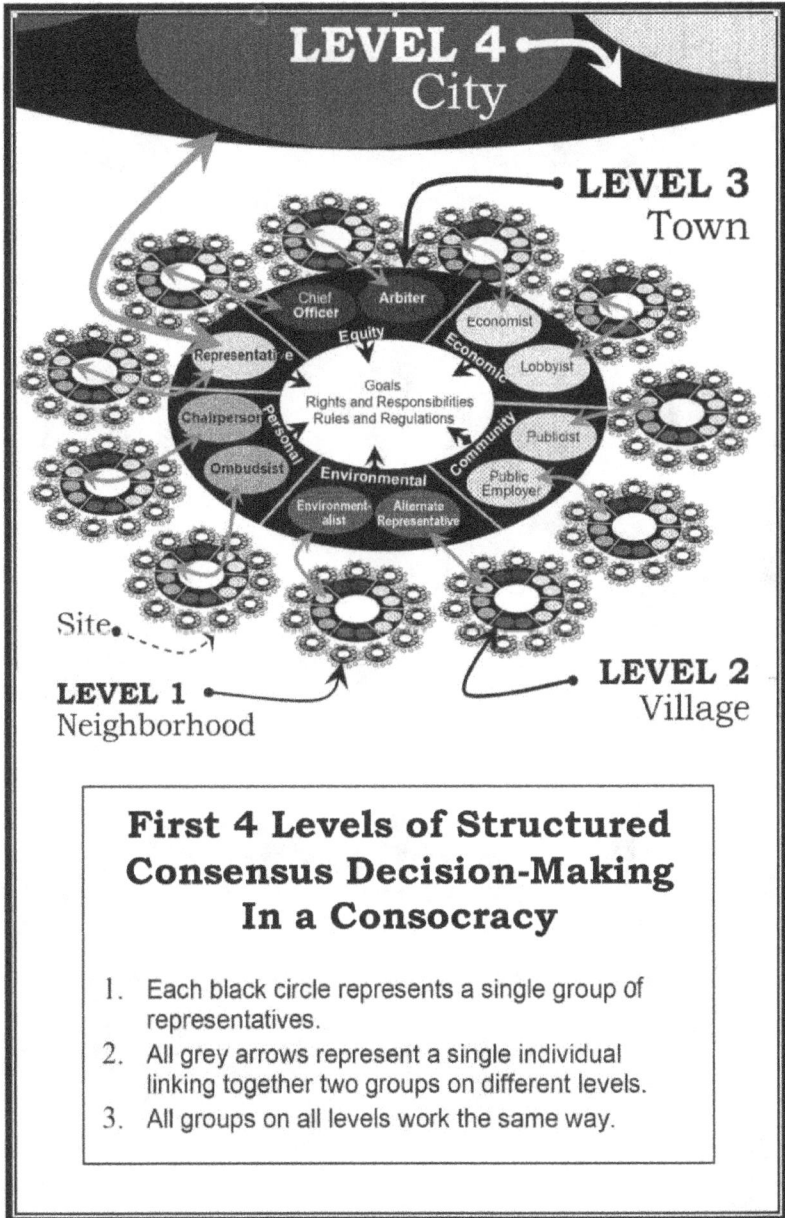

LEVEL 4
City

LEVEL 3
Town

LEVEL 2
Village

LEVEL 1
Neighborhood

Site

Chief Officer · Arbiter · Economist · Representative · Lobbyist · Chairperson · Ombudsist · Publicist · Public Employer · Environmentalist · Alternate Representative

Equity · Economic · Community · Environmental · Personal

Goals
Rights and Responsibilities
Rules and Regulations

First 4 Levels of Structured Consensus Decision-Making In a Consocracy

1. Each black circle represents a single group of representatives.
2. All grey arrows represent a single individual linking together two groups on different levels.
3. All groups on all levels work the same way.

The Consocratic Plan

By TED WELLS

Part 1.   Plan Commencement:

1.1. In this plan, all words in CAPITAL LETTERS LIKE THIS are specifically defined in Part 8 and have meanings that may be different from their customary meaning.

1.2. This plan, either in its entirety or any specified part, shall commence upon agreement by CONSENSUS of the REPRESENTATIVES of all people it AFFECTS.

1.3. All GOALS, PRINCIPES, RIGHTS, RESPONSIBILITIES and RULES, under this plan as they pertain to AFFECTED PUBLIC LAND, and its occupants shall take effect on commencement of this plan.

1.4. All GOALS, PRINCIPLES, RIGHTS, RESPONSIBILITIES and RULES under this plan as they pertain to AFFECTED PRIVATE LAND and its occupants shall take effect on commencement of this plan only when either:

1.4.1.   The occupants of the PRIVATE LAND consent for it to take effect, or

1.4.2.   The rights of an INDIVIDUAL on PRIVATE LAND have been or are imminently likely to be breached, or

1.4.3.   An ACTIVITY on PRIVATE LAND AFFECTS the ENVIRONMENT outside the SITE on which it is located,

Part 2.   Consocratic Principles:

2.1. A CONSOCRACY shall serve the personal and collective interests of all people, managed by the people, for the people.

2.2. Some CONSOCRATIC decisions may be voluntarily delegated to REPRESENTATIVES chosen by CONSENSUS.

2.3. All CONSOCRATIC decisions shall be made only after comprehensively considering the EFFECTS of the proposed change on all relevant PERSONAL, ECONOMIC, EQUITY, COMMUNITY and ENVIRONMENTAL RIGHTS AND RESPONSIBILITIES.

2.4. INDIVIDUALS (and where relevant their families and HOUSEHOLDS), rather than races, cultures, states or religions, shall be the fundamental building block of a CONSOCRACY. Within reason, every person on PRIVATE LAND shall be free to do what he or she chooses provided no other individual's rights are affected and the environment outside that PRIVATE LAND is not affected.

2.5. All public decisions shall be made by CONSENSUS rather than by majority vote. CONSENSUS does not require unanimous agreement, only that no one shall disagree with a decision.

Part 3. Goals of Humanity

3.1. Life
3.2. Liberty (Freedom)
3.3. Happiness
3.4. Health
3.5. Love (Tolerance)
3.6. Community (Friendship)
3.7. Purpose (Work)
3.8. Wisdom (Morality)
3.9. Justice (Honesty)
3.10. Security (Trust)
3.11. Peace
3.12. Environmental sustainability

Part 4. Rights and Responsibilities:

4.1 To achieve the Goals of Humanity set out in Part 3 above, every INDIVIDUAL and GROUP must agree to abide by the following set of RIGHTS AND RESPONSIBILITIES. Amendments to them may be made in the following ways:

4.1.1. **Those RIGHTS AND RESPONSIBILITIES listed below in bold Bookman style type like this are considered fundamental to the operation of a CONSOCRACY and may be amended or deleted only by the CONSENSUS of the TOPMOST GROUP. They often include the verb "shall" dictating a right or responsibility.**

4.1.2. Those RIGHTS AND RESPONSIBILITIES listed below in normal Arial type like this are considered important to the operation of a CONSOCRACY but may be temporarily amended or suspended by the CONSENSUS of any GROUP until conflicting views are resolved. They often include the verb "should" suggesting rather than dictating a right or responsibility.

4.1.3. *Those RIGHTS AND RESPONSIBILITIES listed below in light italic Book Antigua Style type like this have no status initially. They are listed to raise questions for future consideration by all GROUPS as their adoption in some form would help ensure that humanity survives the mess it is currently in.*

4.1.4. Those FUNDAMENTAL RIGHTS AND RESPONSIBILTIES listed in bold type that are not discussed in Chapters 11-15 have been taken directly from the United Nations or Islamic Declarations of Human Rights. They are preceded in this plan by an asterisk (*)

4.1.5. Any RIGHT and RESPONSIBILITY may be clarified by the addition of REGULATIONS created by any Group, provided that the original meaning of the RIGHT, RESPONSIBILITY or RULE is not altered.

4.2. Personal Rights and Resposibilities

4.2.1. Life and Liberty

4.2.1.1. *Every INDIVIDUAL has the right to life, liberty and security.

4.2.1.2. *Human life is sacred and inviolable and every effort shall be made to protect it. In particular no one shall be exposed to injury or death, except under the authority of the Law and even after death the sanctity of a person's body shall be inviolable.

4.2.1.3. *INDIVIDUALS are born free and equal in dignity, rights [and responsibilities set out in this Part 4]. They are endowed with reason and conscience and should act towards one another in a spirit of brotherhood.

4.2.1.4. *Every INDIVIDUAL is entitled to all rights [and responsibilities set out in this Part 4] without distinction of any kind, such as race, color, sex, language, religion, political or other opinion, national or social origin, property, birth or other status.

4.1.1.5. *No distinction shall be made on the basis of the political, jurisdictional or international status of the country, territory or GROUP to which an INDIVIDUAL belongs.

4.2.2. Fertility

4.2.2.1. *Motherhood and childhood are entitled to special care and assistance.

4.2.2.2. *All children, whether born in or out of wedlock, shall enjoy the same social protection.

- - Possible Rights and Responsibilities for future thought No status:-

4.2.2.3. *Every INDIVIDUAL has complete control over his or her own fertility prior to conception.*

4.2.2.4. *A woman has complete control over her own pregnancy during the first three months after conception, including the choice of termination.*

4.2.2.5. *A woman may terminate a pregnancy during the fourth and fifth month after conception only after receiving advice from the father, a medical practitioner, the church (if a member) and her family.*

4.2.2.6. *No one other than the mother, not even the biological father or the government, has the right to force either termination or continuation of a pregnancy at any point. However, the mother must make every effort to notify the biological father in writing of his paternity before the end of the third month of her pregnancy or he shall have no obligation to help raise and provide for the child until it is an adult. (Note the alternative means of public support provided to solo mothers as set out in Part 4.5.6 p367)*

4.2.2.7. *No pregnancy may be intentionally terminated later than five months after conception unless the mother's life is at risk.*

**Possible future "Fundamental Right and responsibility"
for population control:**

4.2.2.8. **[Any child may be removed for adoption at birth if both the mother and father of the child each already has a registered child of his or her own and neither parent has found a childless adult willing to forgo his or her right to have a child by registering the child as a surrogate child to one of the parents.]**

4.2.3. Voluntary Euthanasia

Possible Rights and Responsibilities for future thought - No status: -

4.2.3.1. Any ADULT may choose voluntary euthanasia provided he or she has signed a "living will" at least one year prior to the date of its implementation, and either is terminally ill, is in permanent pain or is comatose.

4.2.3.2. Any other use of Voluntary Euthanasia may occur only with the written consensus of a licensed doctor, a licensed psychiatrist and the closest living relative, e.g. spouse or parent.

4.2.4. Elderly Care

4.2.4.1. It should be the right of anyone over the age of 65 to have access to adequate housing, food and healthcare, and all elderly should be encouraged to continue to participate in society indefinitely, although depending on the person's health and ability the provision of basic resources may require some individually appropriate WORK.

4.2.5. Sensory Perception

4.2.5.1 Detailed, consistent labeling is required on all products and images that are likely to be seen, used or consumed by more than 1000 people. Labeling must include image manipulation and product history prior to public use, including date, origin, location, ingredients/nutrition per 100 gms/mls, and production methods including organic and free range, radiation treatment and genetic modification.

4.2.6. Pleasure Drugs and Gambling

4.2.6.1. **It is illegal for any person to engage in consensus decision-making with any measurable amount of pleasure drug in his or her body or when otherwise under the effects of an illusion producing drug or activity.**

No status:- - Possible Rights and Responsibilities for future thought -

4.2.6.2. Use of drugs with only minor effects, such as caffeine, nicotine, chat and beetle nut, as well as computer gaming, are permitted without restriction, provided any public impact of their use is avoided (such as cigarette smoke, cigarette butts and public spitting of beetle nut in public places).

4.2.6.3. Use of drugs which can significantly alter the mind, such as alcohol, opium, crack, etc, as well as gambling, are permitted only within SAFE SITES, where the user cannot leave that SAFE SITE until all signs of mind alteration have ceased.

4.2.6.4. A SAFE SITE for pleasure drug use may include a private home, business or even a defined public area where appropriate drug use sensors or other controls are installed to keep a person under the influence from leaving the SAFE SITE. It may also include a VEHICLE provided it is never operated under the control of anyone who is under the influence of any illusion or pleasure drug.

4.2.7. Prostitution and Pornography

- Possible Rights and Responsibilities for future thought - -No status:-

4.2.7.1. Only voluntary prostitution involving ADULTS, is permitted, and only if it occurs on an identified SAFE SITE, where no sign of the ACTIVITY or of those participating in it are visible from outside the SAFE SITE.

4.2.7.2. Participation in and access to pornography that does not degrade anyone or involve anyone under 21 is permitted within any SITE provided no sign of the activity or material is visible from outside the SITE.

4.2.8. Nudity and Body Coverings

- - Possible Rights and Responsibilities for future thought - No status:

4.2.8.1. Any level of nudity is permitted on a privately owned SITE or on a clearly identified public SITE, provided it cannot be seen from outside that SITE.

4.2.8.2. Wearing bathing costumes and other light dress that does not expose breasts and genitals is permitted on private property and on clearly identified public properties such as public beaches, resort areas and private clubs.

4.2.8.3. 4.2.8.3. *Any other form of public nudity is not permitted in any other area, including in the media, unless such exposure is strictly controlled and visible only to consenting ADULTS.*

4.2.9. Marriage and Sexual Partnerships

4.2.9.1. *ADULT Men and women, without any limitation due to race, nationality or religion, have the right to marry and to create a family. They are entitled to equal rights as to marriage, during marriage and at its dissolution.

4.2.9.2. *Marriage shall be entered into only with the free and full consent of the intending partners.

4.2.9.3. *ADULT Men and women have the right to divorce without giving reason, after two years separation.

4.2.9.4. *The family is a natural unit of society and is entitled to protection by society and government.

:- - Possible Rights and Responsibilities for future thought - -No status

4.2.9.5. Multiple partnerships are permitted with the same rights and responsibilities as marriages involving only two people.

4.2.9.6. Same-sex partnerships are permitted with the same rights and responsibilities as heterosexual marriages.

4.2.10. Discrimination

4.2.10.1. *It is illegal to discriminate between INDIVIDUALS based on race, color, sex, language, religion, opinion, origin, property, birth or other status.

4.2.10.2. It is illegal for any consequence of discrimination or a product of a discriminatory practice to affect or be sold to anyone outside the area where that discriminatory practice occurs.

- - Possible Rights and Responsibilities for future thought - No status

4.2.10.3. It is every person's right to hold opinions and prejudices of any kind and to express them anywhere at any time, provided no visual, aural or electronic enhancements are utilized, e.g. loud speakers, projection equipment, posters or other printed or broadcast media.

4.2.10.4. Any use of visual, aural or electronic enhancements, including broadcast media to express an opinion or prejudice in public is not a right, but a privilege, which may be limited to publicly defined areas or times if it physically, visually or aurally involves OFFENSIVE OR OBJECTIONABLE behavior, activities or material.

4.2.10.5. OFFENSIVE OR OBJECTIONABLE use of the internet, cell phones, home delivered mail and other forms of private communication are prohibited.

4.2.11. Mental, Physical, Social Disabilities

4.2.11.1. It is the right of every disabled person to actively participate in society to the extent their disability allows them, and to have reasonable housing, food, healthcare and necessary tools provided, although provision of these things may require some WORK from the person according to his or her health and ability.

4.2.12. Violence And Abuse

4.2.12.1. Physical, mental and social VIOLENCE or ABUSE in any form on anyone of any age is prohibited.

4.2.12.2. Anyone considered by a GROUP to have been violent or abusive to others may be subject to periods of social isolation while being rehabilitated.

4.2.12.3. Anyone who is considered violent or abusive may be removed from participating in any group

decision-making by the consensus of the remaining members of that group

4.2.13. Obesity

- - Possible Rights and Responsibilities for future thought - No status

4.2.13.1. Free professional health advice and assistance should be provided to those who are obese.

4.2.13.2. The advertising of heavily processed, fatty or high sugar content foods or of any shop or restaurant selling or serving only such foods is prohibited.

4.2.13.3. Disproportionately taxing the sale of heavily processed, fatty or high sugar content foods in shops or restaurants to recover public health costs of the obese is permitted.

4.2.14. Privacy

4.2.14.1. *No one shall be subjected to arbitrary interference with his privacy, family, home or correspondence, nor to attacks upon his or her honor and reputation. Every INDIVIDUAL has the right to the protection of the law against such interference or attacks.

4.2.14.2. A globally unique personal identification code that is associated with a clearly defined, globally unique place on this planet is required for every living individual and every subsequent live birth.

4.2.14.3. Every person who uses any public land or any public service, conducts a business or engages in government consensus decision-making must provide this code to public authorities if officially requested to do so in writing.

4.2.14.4. It is illegal to disclose, or use for any private or commercial purpose any personal information using the unique IDENTIFICATION CODE of

INDIVIDUALS, with the exception that all public authorities may internally cross link information on INDIVIDUALS using this code.

4.2.14.5. Every INDIVIDUAL has the right to visual, aural and spatial privacy within a HOUSEHOLD.

4.2.14.6. On PRIVATE LAND, the audio or visual surveillance, scanning, recording, photography and/or tracking of anyone without a court order or the INDIVIDUAL'S written consent is prohibited.

4.2.14.7. On PUBLIC LAND, the unobtrusive surveillance, scanning, recording, photography and/or tracking of anyone is permitted.

4.2.15. Private Property

4.2.15.1. *Every INDIVIDUAL has the right to own and utilize private property alone as well as in association with others, although this may require WORK to pay for it.

4.2.15.2. Every INDIVIDUAL has the right to the temporary protection of the moral and material interests resulting from any scientific, literary or artistic production of which he or she is the author.

4.2.15.3. *No one shall be arbitrarily deprived of his property.

4.2.15.4. It is illegal to own, buy, or sell another human being.

4.2.15.5. It is illegal to control the thoughts or actions of an ADULT unless that ADULT is convicted of an offence for which incarceration and/or education is the punishment and/or rehabilitation is required.

Possible Rights and Responsibilities for future thought - No status

4.2.15.6. *Exclusive rights to use and/or duplicate an original idea or object is permitted for five years after its creation, or for the length of time necessary to recover one hundred times the cost of creating the original idea or object, which ever is less.*

4.2.16. Carrying Arms

4.2.16.1. It is illegal to privately make, possess or use any nuclear, chemical, biological or laser weapon, or any bomb, missile or other implement designed to injure, torture or kill other than a non-automatic rifle.

4.2.16.2. It should be illegal to privately own or use any gun other than a non-automatic rifle outside a designated SAFE SITE, including a handgun, automatic rifle or machine gun

- Possible Rights and Responsibilities for future thought - No status:

4.2.16.3. *It is the right of every ADULT to privately own any number of non-lethal hand weapons including pepper spray, tasers and multi purpose folding pocket-knives.*

4.2.16.4. *It is the right of every ADULT to privately own one rifle as well as two hunting knives provided the rifle cannot fire automatically and no weapons are concealed when carried in public.*

4.2.17. Access to Water, Food and Shelter

4.2.17.1. It is the right of every INDIVIDUAL to reside within a HOUSEHOLD either alone or in the company of others with their mutual consent.

4.2.17.2. It is the right of every INDIVIDUAL to have sufficient water to live healthily, including water for drinking, bathing and, where possible, for growing food crops for personal and family consumption, although this may require reasonable WORK according to a person's health and ability. The use of water for any commercial purpose is not a right.

4.2.17.3. It is the right of every INDIVIDUAL to have adequate food to live on, although this may require reasonable WORK according to a person's health and ability.

4.2.17.4. It is the right of every ADULT to be able to voluntarily occupy sufficient exclusive private three-dimensional sheltered space with access to sunlight and natural air, to allow that person to stand and lie down with limbs fully extended in any direction (approximately 500 ft^3 or 15 m^3 of three-dimensional space with a minimum dimension of 8 feet or 2.4 metres), although this may require reasonable work according to a person's health and ability.

4.3. Economic Rights and Resposibilities

4.3.1. The Market Place

4.3.1.1. **It is the right of every INDIVIDUAL and GROUP to participate in the MARKET PLACE provided such activity does does not interfere with either SOCIAL JUSTICE or ENVIRONMENTAL SUSTAINABILITY.**

4.3.2. Work

4.3.2.1. ***Every ADULT has the right to WORK, to free choice of employment, to just and favorable conditions of WORK and to protection against unemployment.**

4.3.2.2. ***Every INDIVIDUAL, without any discrimination, has the right to equal pay for equal WORK.**

4.3.2.3. ***Every INDIVIDUAL has the right to form and to join trade unions for the protection of his interests.**

4.3.2.4. ***It is the right of every INDIVIDUAL to earn sufficient income to live and raise a family in security (including with adequate privacy, water, food and shelter and with access to health and education facilities) through freely chosen WORK under just, non-exploitive conditions.**

4.3.2.5. **Where WORK in the private sector is unavailable, it is the right of every INDIVIDUAL seeking WORK to be provided WORK at a reasonable LIVING WAGE improving public roads, parks, public utilities, schools, health facilities, the arts or in other areas of public responsibility appropriate to their health and ability, and as far as practicable in an area of their interest.**

4.3.2.6. **Every INDIVIDUAL has the right to rest and**

leisure, including reasonable limitation of working hours and periodic holidays with pay.

4.3.3. Job Sharing

- Possible Rights and Responsibilities for future thought - No status -

4.3.3.1. Full time job sharing between two or more people over a 4 to 24 hour day, two to seven day week is encouraged to promote better work opportunities, social cohesion, cooperation and use of natural and physical resources.

4.3.4 Corporations

4.3.5.1. Every INDIVIDUAL, GROUP or ENTERPRISE should have the right to establish and manage a CORPORATION provided that for each CORPORATION, a group of living people capable at all times of paying for all liabilities, including any negative impact of the CORPORATION and its operations, products and services on humanity and the ENVIRONMENT, accepts full responsibility for it.

4.3.5.2. All owners and managers of a CORPORATION charged with a crime should be personally liable and punishable for any corporate guilt proven in a court of law.

4.3.5. Cooperatives

4.3.6.1. Every INDIVIDUAL, GROUP or ENTERPRISE should have the right to establish and manage Cooperatives. They are the only form of business that may be operated in the MARKET PLACE without the express consent of the GROUP responsible for the area where they operate.

4.3.6.2. INDIVIDUALS and others who live together on a single SITE and who completely own and run their own business solely from that SITE, operate a COOPERATIVE by definition, regardless of the actual formal structure of that business. (E.g. farmers, home occupations, local shopkeepers who live over their shops, etc.)

4.3.6. Currency

- Possible Rights and Responsibilities for future thought - No status -

4.3.4.1. A universal currency should be adopted by all on the planet as soon as practicable.

4.3.7. Loans, Interest and inflation

4.3.7.1. It should be illegal for individuals and businesses to charge a time-based fee, or interest, on borrowed money.

4.3.7.2. It should be the right of every INDIVIDUAL, GROUP or ENTERPRISE to charge a fixed fee on borrowed money provided that the fee does not increase over time and does not exceed the amount of money that the fee would increase through inflation over a ten year period in the locality where the fee is charged.

4.3.8. Tax Avoidance and Money Laundering

4.3.8.1. Bank accounts in all countries should be accessible to all authorized government officials all of the time.

4.3.8. Money laundering is illegal and any account involved in money laundering should, as far as practicable, have its contents confiscated by the government were the money originated.

4.3.9. Limited Liability

4.3.9.1. When an ENTERPRISE ceases to operate for any reason and leaves any debt owing, that debt should, become the personal debt of all directors, and other owners (including stock/share holders) that were involved in that ENTERPRISE in proportion to their investment in that ENTERPRISE over the previous three years prior to its closure.

4.3.10. Bankruptcy

4.3.10.1. Anyone unable to repay a debt should be declared a "Bankrupt" until the debt is paid in full or until ten years has passed, which ever is less.

4.3.10.2. Anyone declared a "Bankrupt" should be required to include the title "Bankrupt" or "Br." before his or her name whenever it is spoken in public used in the media or included in any written correspondence.

4.3.10.3. No person declared bankrupt or within five years of its termination should be able to own or manage a business.

4.4. Equity Rights and Responsibilities

4.4.1. Government

4.4.1.1. *Every ADULT has the right to take part in his own governance through freely chosen REPRESENTATIVES.

4.4.1.2. *The will of all the people shall be the basis of the authority of government.

4.4.1.3. *In the exercise of his or her RIGHTS AND RESPONSIBILITIES, Every INDIVIDUAL is subject only to such limitations as are determined by law solely for the purpose of securing due recognition and respect for the RIGHTS AND RESPONSIBILITIES and of meeting the just requirements of morality, public order and the general welfare of society.

4.4.1.4. The role of Government is to guarantee public enjoyment of their rights and responsibilities as set forth in this Part 4: RIGHTS AND RESPONSIBILITIES.

4.4.1.5. All decision-making shall consider PERSONAL, ECONOMIC, EQUITY, COMMUNITY and ENVIRONMENTAL SYSTEMS of change.

4.4.1.6. The RIGHTS AND RESPONSIBILITIES set out in this Part 4 may not be exercised contrary to the GOALS of HUMANITY set out in Part 2.

4.4.1.7. Nothing in this PLAN may be interpreted as implying for any INDIVIDUAL or GROUP except the TOPMOST GROUP, any right to engage in any ACTIVITY or to perform any act aimed at the removal of any of the RIGHTS AND RESPONSIBILITIES set forth herein.

4.4.1.8. Public government decision-making

must:

4.4.1.8.1. Enable many autonomous communities to live in the same area together peacefully,

4.4.1.8.2. Remove the use or threat of force to resolve inter-community differences,

4.4.1.8.3. Remove the ability of narcissists to buy their selection as political representatives,

4.4.1.8.4. Remove the influence of social media and fake news from all political decisions,

4.4.1.8.5. Ensure environmental and social impacts are considered in all political decisions,

4.4.1.8.6. Ensure that there is gender equality in all political decisions,

4.4.1.8.7. Ensure community representatives are personally known to all those who select them.

4.4.1.8.8. Ensure everyone, including minorities, are considered equally in all political decisions

4.4.1.8.9. Avoid election cycles which force short term solutions to long term problems

4.4.1.8.10. Ensure the rapid, peaceful implementation of all political decisions

4.4.2. Red Tape Makers

4.4.2.1. Both administrative staff and public decision-makers should immediately remove themselves from involvement in any public decision in which they, a family member, a personal friend or a business associate has an interest.

4.4.2.2. An annually updated register of all public servants, including administrative staff and public decision-makers, containing not only educational background and work experience, but more personal information such as family members, hobbies, club memberships, personal goals, philosophy of life, reason for interest in public issues, criminal record and other relevant matters, should be available to the public at all times.

4.4.3. Planning

4.4.3.1. The six part planning process shall be a fundamental, fully transparent component of every public decision, which:

4.4.3.1.1. Identifies what the future state should be; that is, sets the goals,

4.4.3.1.2. Identifies and clarifies the problems that may interfere with achieving these goals, and the opportunities that may achieve them quicker or with fewer resources,

4.4.3.1.3. Identifies and analyses (including side effects) alternative ways to solve the problems and utilize the opportunities to achieve the goals,

4.4.3.1.4. Chooses the best way to do this; that is, comes up with a "Plan",

4.4.3.1.5. Implements "The Plan",

4.4.3.1.6. Monitors subsequent change and if the results are not as expected, revises "The Plan" (or alternatively, modifies the goals).

4.4.4. Taking

4.4.4.1. Any PUBLIC TAKING of PRIVATE PROPERTY or other private rights should result in a significant benefit to the general public that is not achievable any other way or in any other place at less human cost.

4.4.4.2. Any personal loss from a PUBLIC TAKING should be fairly compensated including for the time and trauma of replacing or experiencing the loss.

4.4.4.3. The value of any loss incurred in a PUBLIC TAKING should not include any improvements proposed by the owner of PRIVATE PROPERTY or undertaken by the owner after being formally informed of the public TAKING.

4.4.5. Taxes

- Possible Rights and Responsibilities for future thought - No status -

4.4.5.1. Taxes based on income and profit should be phased out over the long term in favor of "value added" taxes based on the exchange of all goods and services except the sale of the main family home.

4.4.5.2. "Value Added" Taxes or GST should be paid on every financial transaction, including the movement of money or other financial assets, such as stocks and bonds, from any account to any other.

4.4.5.3. With the exception of basic public mobility, education, healthcare and justice services, individuals and businesses that use public utilities and services should pay for them as far as practicable directly though the use of a two tiered monetary system that uses GST receipts on "necessities" to pay for them.

4.4.5.4. There should be taxes on all POLLUTION and on the use or removal of non-renewable RESOURCES, such as minerals and petroleum.

4.4.5.5. There should be no taxes on rural land, only on the sale of any products or services that it provides or generates.

4.4.6. Measurement and Language

- Possible Rights and Responsibilities for future thought - No status -

4.4.6.1. The metric system of weights and measures should be adopted by all as soon as practicable.

4.4.6.2. As far as practicable, individuals and businesses should be encouraged to help develop and use computer assisted electronic equipment that allows the translation of all communication into the local language of both the speaker and listener, rather than encourage or force the disuse of any particular minority language.

4.4.7. Censorship

4.4.7.1. All censorship should be prohibited except when ordered by a court, or in the following circumstances:

4.4.7.1.1. To protect the privacy of an INDIVIDUAL acting within the law when on private land.

4.4.7.1.2. To protect the health and wellbeing of those under the age of twenty one

4.4.7.1.3. To protect the rights of those accused of a crime.

4.4.7.1.4. To protect the safety of INDIVIDUALS who are in imminent life-threatening danger. Note: This part (4.4.7.1.4) may be invoked temporarily prior to police actions against suspected criminals.

4.4.7.2. Anyone breaching these censorship rules may be held criminally liable for any financial, physical or mental costs incurred as a result of that breach.

4.4.8. Armed Forces, Police, Terrorism and War

4.4.8.1.. Internal local police forces should be the only permanent law enforcement agency permitted anywhere, although as part of the police force there may be departments staffed to rapidly deploy trained paid volunteers for external defense and to respond to any internal or external natural or man-made emergencies.

4,4.8.2. Police forces should be armed only when required to ensure public safety or their own.

4.4.8.3. Every police force should be structured, staffed, trained and funded so that all staff spend at least 10% of their time every year undertaking activities that enhance peace without the use of force, such as rebuilding internal or external public services and facilities after a natural disaster, educating the poor or constructing low cost housing.

I4.4.8.4. Adults of any age or gender may participate in the internal or external peace enhancing activities of the police force without having to participate in its enforcement activities.

4.4.9. Pacifism

4.4.9.1. *Every INDIVIDUAL has an obligation to preserve and maintain peace, and to resolve differences of opinion peacefully without physical or mental violence.

4.4.9.2. *Every INDIVIDUAL has the right to defend him or herself, family or friends against injury to people or property within his or her own SITE.

4.4.9.3. All people have the right to refuse to kill or to participate in armed aggression or armed defense.

4.4.9.4. Every INDIVIDUAL has the right to passively resist participating in any ACTIVITY that breaches a PRINCIPLE, RIGHT, RESPONSIBILITY, RULE or REGULATION in this Plan.

4.4.10. The Law

4.4.10.1. All laws, including "common laws" should be set down in writing and guilt proven through the presentation of evidence with clear and direct reference to that written law,

4.4.10.2. Plea bargaining in any form should be prohibited.

4.4.11. Justice, Lawyers and Experts:

4.4.11.1. *Every INDIVIDUAL has the right to recognition everywhere as a person before the law.

4.4.11.2. *All INDIVIDUALS are equal before the law and are entitled without any DISCRIMINATION to equal protection of the law against any DISCRIMINATION in violation of these RIGHTS AND RESPONSIBILITIES and against any incitement to such discrimination.

4.4.11.3. *No INDIVIDUAL shall be subjected to torture, cruelty or inhuman treatment in mind or body, or degraded, or threatened with injury either to him or herself or to anyone related to or held

dear by him or her, or forcibly made to confess to the commission of a crime, or forced to consent to an act which is injurious to his or her interests.

4.4.11.4. *Every INDIVIDUAL has the right to protect his or her honor and reputation against calumnies, groundless charges or deliberate attempts at defamation and blackmail.

4.4.11.5. *Every INDIVIDUAL has the right to an effective remedy for acts violating the fundamental rights granted him or her by law.

4.4.11.6. *No one shall be subjected to arbitrary arrest, detention or exile.

4.4.11.7. *Every INDIVIDUAL is entitled in full equality to a fair and public hearing by an independent and impartial tribunal, in the determination of his RIGHTS AND RESPONSIBILITIES and of any criminal charge against him.

4.4.11.8. *Every INDIVIDUAL charged with a penal offence has the right to be presumed innocent until proved guilty according to law in a public trial at which he has had all the guarantees necessary for his defense, or until guilt is voluntarily admitted.

4.4.11.9. *No INDIVIDUAL shall be held guilty of any penal offence on account of any act or omission which did not constitute a penal offence, under national or international law, at the time when it was committed. Nor shall a heavier penalty be imposed than the one that was applicable at the time the penal offence was committed.

4.4.11.10. *Every individual is responsible for his or her actions. Responsibility for a crime cannot be vicariously extended to other members of his or

her family or GROUP, who are not otherwise involved in the commission of the crime in question.

- Possible Rights and Responsibilities for future thought- No status -

4.4.11.11. All civil and criminal Court cases should use a "Restorative Justice" system with a jury of up to 12 peers in which there are an equal number of the jurors known to the victim and to the defendant. (including parents or other relatives if appropriate.)

4.4.11.12. The jury should be led by an independent judge acting as a Mediator chosen jointly by the victim and the defendant.

4.4.11.13. Evidence to establish guilt or innocence should be presented by the police as they do now, but this would occur through the Mediator

4.4.11.14. With the guidance of the Mediator/Judge, the jury should reach a consensus decision which not only considers the guilt or innocence of the defendant, but clearly identifies the harm that has been done by the criminal activity.

4.4.11.15. With the guidance of the Mediator/Judge, the jury's decision should also both identify how the harm will be repaired and how the offender will be rehabilitated.

4.4.11.16. Court proceeding should be as informal as possible with any "expert" evidence from any party vetted and introduced to the Jury by the Mediator and any Legal advice given to any party should occur before or after formal jury meetings, not during them unless allowed by the Mediator.

4.4.12. Punishment:

4.4.12.1. *No INDIVIDUAL may be subjected to torture or capital punishment although temporary mechanical or electronic restraint of the offender may be appropriate for certain offences.

4.4.12.2. Beyond fair compensation to the victim(s) for any loss (including temporary or permanent physical or mental damage, but not including

punitive damage) incurred, behavioral change shall be the sole focus of an offender's punishment and for determining his or her release back into society.

4.5. Community Rights and Resposibilities

4.5.1. Public Media and Fake News

4.5.1.1. It is the right of every INDIVIDUAL in every GROUP to have full time access to publicly funded news MEDIA (television, radio and the internet) which are meticulously free of political or commercial advertising and biased or fake content.

4.5.2. Public Health Care, Pandemics

4.5.2.1. It should be the right of every INDIVIDUAL to have access to GROUP subsidized public health care, although minimum INDIVIDUAL payments may require reasonable WORK according to a person's health and ability.

4.5.3. Public Education

4.5.3.1. *Every INDIVIDUAL has the right to education. Education shall be free, at least in the elementary and fundamental stages. Technical and professional education shall be made generally available and higher education shall be equally accessible to all on the basis of merit.

4.5.3.2. *Education shall be directed to the full development of the human personality and to the strengthening of respect for human rights and fundamental freedoms. It shall promote understanding, tolerance and friendship among all nations, racial or religious groups, and shall further the activities of any CONSOCRACY or other GROUP for the maintenance of peace.

4.5.3.3. *Parents have a prior right to choose the kind of education that shall be given to their children.

4.5.3.4. *Pursuit of knowledge and search after truth is not only a right but a duty.

- Possible Rights and Responsibilities for future thought - No status -

4.5.3.5. *Education should focus on teacher guided, self- motivated and individually tailored learning, with verbal language skills an important early childhood focus.*

4.5.3.6. *Education should be mandatory for all to the age of 16 if local education includes some mandatory instruction in all religions and local languages or alternatively, if all minority groups which make up at least five percent of the local population have their own schools,*

4.5.3.7. *Educational choices should include the opportunity to learn by doing through apprenticeships and trade schools.*

4.5.3.8. *University education should focus on fine-tuning and putting into global context INDIVIDUAL knowledge.*

4.5.4. Religious Persecution

4.5.4.1. *Every INDIVIDUAL has the right to freedom of thought, conscience and religion; this right includes freedom to change his or her religion or belief.

4.5.4.2. It should be a right, but not an obligation, of every INDIVIDUAL to develop and maintain his or her own religious beliefs and to worship among others who share the same beliefs, provided that this is done peacefully and unobtrusively.

4.5.4.3. No INDIVIDUAL should attempt to convert another INDIVIDUAL to a religion or other belief system without that INDIVIDUAL'S expressed prior consent.

4.5.5. Cultural Preservation

4.5.5.1. *Every INDIVIDUAL has the right to a nationality.

4.5.5.2. *No one shall be arbitrarily deprived of his

44

nationality nor denied the right to change his nationality.

4.5.5.3. *Every INDIVIDUAL has the right to freedom of peaceful assembly and association.

4.5.5.4. *No one may be compelled to belong to an ASSOCIATION, ENTERPRISE, INSTITUTION or GROUP.

4.5.5.5. *Every INDIVIDUAL has the right to participate freely in the cultural life of the COMMUNITY, to enjoy the arts and to share in scientific advancement and its benefits.

4.5.5.6. *Every INDIVIDUAL has duties to the COMMUNITY in which they live including recognizing the rights and freedoms of others.

4.5.5.7 It should be the right, but not an obligation, of every INDIVIDUAL to live among others who share the same culture, common symbols, rituals, language and beliefs, provided that it is done peacefully and,

4.5.5.8. It should be the right, but not an obligation, of every INDIVIDUAL to support his or her culture's maintenance and future existence, provided that it is done unobtrusively.

4.5.6. Social Support

4.5.6.1. *Every INDIVIDUAL has the right to social security and is entitled to the economic, social and cultural rights indispensable for his or her dignity and the free development of his or her personality, in accordance with the organization and resources of each GROUP

4.5.6.2. *Every CHILD has the right to be maintained and properly brought up by its parents, and cannot be forced to WORK. If parents are for some reason unable to discharge their obligations towards a CHILD it shall become the responsibility of the

COMMUNITY to fulfil these obligations at public expense.

4.5.6.3. All those who are physically or mentally unable to work in any constructive capacity should be given a LIVING WAGE and have free access to all social support services including health care, water, food and shelter for as long as needed.

4.5.6.4. Where WORK in the private sector is unavailable, it should be the right of every individual seeking work to be provided WORK at a reasonable LIVING WAGE in areas of public responsibility appropriate to their health, skills and ability, and in an area of their interest..

4.5.7. Public Utilities and Services

4.5.7.1. *Every INDIVIDUAL has the right to equal access to PUBLIC UTILITIES AND SERVICES available to others in his COMMUNITY.

4.6. ENVIRONMENT RIGHTS AND RESPOSIBILITIES

4.6.1. Resource Sustainability

4.6.1.1. No human activity, creation or decision may reduce the ability of the natural local or global environment to sustain life.

4.6.1.2. Every INDIVIDUAL has an obligation to preserve and/or regulate the sustainable use of natural and physical resources for future generations.

4.6.2. Climate Change

4.6.2.1. Every human activity, creation and decision shall attempt to reduce green house gas emissions and their effects on global warming as quickly as possible to pre-2000 AD levels

4.6.3. Natural Hazards

4.6.3.1. All INDIVIDUALS, businesses and INSTITUTIONS shall take every reasonable precaution to avoid or minimize their risk of exposure to known natural hazards, including sea level rise, earthquakes, tsunami, volcanic activity, flooding and landslip.

4.6.4. Movement

4.6.4.1. *Every INDIVIDUAL has the right to freedom of movement on PUBLIC PATHS.

4.6.4.2. *Every INDIVIDUAL has the right to leave any COMMUNITY, including his own, and to return to his COMMUNITY.

4.6.4.3. *Every INDIVIDUAL has the right to seek and to enjoy asylum from persecution in other COMMUNITIES, except in the case of prosecutions

47

genuinely arising from non-political crimes or from acts contrary to the RIGHTS AND RESPONSIBILITIES stated here.

4.6.4.4. Every parcel of PRIVATE LAND shall have free direct access to a PUBLIC PATH such as a public road, public alleyway, public hallway or other accessible part of a public movement network.

4.6.4.5. It is the right of every INDIVIDUAL to be able to move freely between parcels of PUBLIC and/or PRIVATE LAND along PUBLIC PATHS at no personal cost.

4.6.4.6. It is the right of every INDIVIDUAL to be able to move solid objects including VEHICLES between parcels of PUBLIC and/or PRIVATE LAND along PUBLIC PATHS at a cost that is proportionate (in terms of distance, volume, speed, environmental impact, etc.) to his or her use of PUBLIC PATHS.

4.6.4.7. All liquids and gases except those found within their natural environment in their natural state shall be contained at all times and any movement of them shall incur a cost that is proportionate (in terms of distance, volume, speed, environmental impact, etc.) to their use of PUBLIC PATHS.

4.6.4.8. All transmissions, diseases and pollution shall be controlled in a manner that stops their EFFECTS beyond the boundary of the SITE where they are generated or beyond the SITE boundaries of the GROUP(s) that permits them.

4.6.5. Transportation Network

4.6.5.1. Public roads should be arranged as part of a comprehensive, integrated public transportation network involving a hierarchy of road sizes and purposes along with extensive but separate rail, air, bicycle and pedestrian transportation systems.

4.6.5.2. Until fully carbon neutral transportation systems are developed, public rail transport should be the principal means of movement of people and goods overland between COMMUNITIES and for the movement of people within large intensively developed COMMUNITIES

4.6.6. Nodal Growth

4.6.6.1. PUBLIC FACILITIES AND SERVICES such as schools, medical facilities and local shops should be encouraged to cluster together in NODES wherever possible, preferably around public rail transportation terminals.

4.6.6.2. The density of URBAN DEVELOPMENT and habitation should increase as far as practicable closer to clustered PUBLIC FACILITIES AND SERVICES and rail transportation terminals.

4.6.6.3. The most intensively developed areas should include multi-use public gathering places linked together by pedestrian only PATHS.

4.6.6.4. Private VEHICLE movement, ACCESS and parking within the center of densely developed NODES should be underground or otherwise isolated from ground level pedestrian PATHS. .

4.6.7. Effects Based Development Control

4.6.7.1. All development shall minimize health and safety risks to life, such as uncontrolled fire, flooding, building collapse, injury and disease.

4.6.7.2. All development shall avoid, remedy or mitigate all EFFECTS of development on the ENVIRONMENT.

4.6.7.3. All development on public land shall be planned using the 6-part process identified 4.4.3 above.

4.6.7.4. On any SITE, the use, location, scale and arrangement of development may only be limited where the impact of such development is likely to AFFECT the ENVIRONMENT (including people) beyond the boundaries of that SITE or interfere with the future needs of other COMMUNITIES and GROUPS.

4.6.8. Rural Land Use

4.6.8.1. Class. 1, 2, and 3 land, that is, flat to gently rolling well drained land with stable foundations and good topsoil should be permanently protected for plant and animal production, except in the following circumstances:

4.6.8.1.1. When used for urban growth and/or the provision of necessary public utilities, facilities and services, including the public transportation network if, following an analysis of all alternative options discussed in free and open public gatherings, it is determined there are no other practicable options,

4.6.8.1.2. When used for housing for those involved in the sustainable use of rural land when other Class land is not available nearby,

4.6.8.1.3. When used for the removal and processing of local non-renewable resources, if following an analysis of all alternative options discussed in free and open public gatherings, it is determined there are no other practicable options.

4.6.8.2. Any use of rural land under clause 4.6.8.1.3 above should incur a resource use charge not less than the maximum existing open sky food production on equivalent nearby land, until the land is again capable of such food production.

4.6.9. Land Banking

4.6.9.1. All COMMUNITIES experiencing high growth or decay should consider PUBLIC LAND BANKING to improve growth management and PLANNING and to ensure any increase in LAND value due to such change is primarily realized by the PUBLIC rather than by speculative PRIVATE LAND owners.

4.6.10. Energy

4.6.10.1. All use of naturally occurring coal, oil, natural gas, and other carbon based fuels shall be phased out of PUBLIC use as soon as practicable.

4.6.10.2. Any existing ACTIVITY that requires carbon based fuels shall convert to other forms of fuel or utilize carbon-based fuels created from processed recently grown plant material.

4.6.10.3. Renewable energy sources, such as the natural movement of wind, river water and tides may be used as sources of energy provided the impact of any conversion equipment or structure on the ENVIRONMENT, including the scenic landscape and local wildlife, has been minimized.

4.6.10.4. Directly utilizing energy from the sun, should be the preferred method of obtaining energy for all human ACTIVITY, provided the impact of any conversion equipment or structure on the ENVIRONMENT, including the scenic landscape and local wildlife, has been minimized.

4.6.11. Pollution and Recycling

4.6.11.1. Any waterborne or airborne POLLUTION, radiation, electronic transmissions or excessive sound or light should be controlled at its source in a manner that limits it from going beyond the boundary of the SITE where it is generated, unless explicitly accepted onto other SITES by those subjected to them.

4.6.11.2. The creator of any potentially environmentally polluting material that leaves the SITE on which it is created, should be responsible for its safe recycling, or permanent containment when it becomes obsolete, unusable or unwanted by others outside that SITE.

4.6.12. Hazardous Substances

4.6.12.1. All public exposure to hazardous substances should be avoided, but if that is not possible and use of the hazardous substance is in the public interest, then all risks should be mitigated to the greatest extent possible.

4.6.12.2. The creation, use, storage and/or transport of hazardous substances should only occur on approved sites that are isolated from the general public, contained in approved vessels and transported in approved vehicles or pipelines along approved routes, and all of the above only if specifically consented following full public disclosure and debate.

4.6.12.3. Where the creation, use, storage and/or transport of a hazardous substance is unavoidable and is a potential hazard to the general public, the hazard should be monitored 24/7 by independent experts with personal experience and knowledge of the hazard, entirely paid for by the creator of the hazard.

Part 5. Fundamental Rules:

5.1. Status of the Rules in this Plan:

5.1.1. No RULE in this PLAN may be modified, added to or deleted without the CONSENSUS of all members of the TOPMOST GROUP.

5.1.2. All modifications, additions and deletions to the RULES of this PLAN made by a TOPMOST GROUP shall revert to their original form and meaning if, through changing circumstances, the GROUP making TOPMOST GROUP decisions is no longer the TOPMOST GROUP, unless the new TOPMOST GROUP by CONSENSUS accepts them.

5.1.3. REGULATIONS may be made to clarify or expand upon any RULE in this PLAN. They may be made by any GROUP for any reason including clarifying the timing of implementation, the methodology of implementation or any other relevant matter, provided the original meaning of the RULE is not altered.

5.2. Status of the Goals, Rights and Responsibilities in this Plan:

5.2.1. Every INDIVIDUAL, HOUSEHOLD, ASSOCIATION, ENTER-PRISE, INSTITUTION and GROUP shall abide by the GOALS set out in Part 3, the RIGHTS AND RESPONSIBILITIES set out in Part 4, the Rules set out in Part 5 and if adopted, Part 6 of this plan.

5.2.2. All RIGHTS AND RESPONSIBILITIES shall apply equally to INDIVIDUALS, HOUSEHOLDS, ASSOCIATIONS, ENTERPRISES, INSTITUTIONS and GROUPS unless there is a clear intention otherwise.

5.2.3. Every right of an INDIVIDUAL has a corresponding responsibility for a GROUP, and every right of a GROUP has a corresponding responsibility for INDIVIDUALS.

5.2.4. There are three types of RIGHTS AND

RESPONSIBILITIES.

5.2.4.1. FUNDAMENTAL RIGHTS AND RESPONSIBILITIES are those that must apply to all INDIVIDUALS and GROUPS to allow a fully operating Consocracy to work and to allow humanity to survive while it cleans up the mess it is in.

5.2.4.2. Some FUNDAMENTAL RIGHTS AND RESPONSIBILITIES listed in Part 4 are already adopted by most countries of the world as part of either the United Nations or Islamic Universal Declaration of Human Rights. These are marked with an asterisk (*).

5.2.4.3. FUNDAMENTAL RIGHTS AND RESPONSIBILITIES are listed in Part 4 above in bold Bookman Style type like this and may be amended or deleted only by the CONSENSUS of the TOPMOST GROUP.

5.2.4.4. RECOMMENDED RIGHTS AND RESPONSIBILITIES are those that should be adopted to encourage peaceful co-existence between people, achieve social justice or promote environmental sustainability. They are not fundamental to the operation of a Consocracy, but they could significantly improve its operation and humanity's chances of survival. They often include the verb "should" or "may" suggesting rather than dictating a right or responsibility.

5.2.4.5. RECOMMENDED RIGHTS AND RESPONSIBILITIES are listed in Part 4 above in light rounded Arial upright type like this and may be temporarily amended or suspended by the CONSENSUS of any GROUP until conflicting views are resolved.

5.2.4.6. POSSIBLE RIGHTS AND RESPONSIBILITIES are those that might be helpful to manage specific GROUPS or help achieve CONSENSUS among divergent opinions. Although they are intended to be relatively neutral, Because of possible religious, cultural, political or other conflicts, they may not be appropriate to use as written in every GROUP.

5.2.4.7. POSSIBLE RIGHTS AND RESPONSIBILITIES are those listed in Part 4 above in light italic Book Antigua style type like this and have no status initially. They are listed to raise questions for future consideration by all GROUPS as their adoption in some form would help ensure the long term survival of humanity.

5.2.5. RIGHTS AND RESPONSIBILITIES may be amended, deleted or added in the following way:

5.2.5.1. Any RIGHT or RESPONSIBILITY may be clarified and expanded upon by the addition of REGULATIONS created by any GROUP. REGULATIONS may detail the timing of its implementation, the methodology of its implementation or any other relevant matter.

5.2.5.2. Any additional RIGHT or RESPONSIBILITY may be added by any GROUP at any time, provided it does not conflict with any existing GOAL, RIGHT, RESPONSIBILITY or RULE.

5.2.5.3. No RIGHT or RESPONSIBILITY in bold type may be modified or deleted without the CONSENSUS of the TOPMOST GROUP.

5.3. Structure of a Consocracy:

5.3.1. A CONSOCRACY uses STRUCTURED CONSENSUS decision-making to reach decisions among large numbers of INDIVIDUALS, which requires:

5.3.1.1. All INDIVIDUALS on a single SITE (usually, but not necessarily a HOUSEHOLD) may choose in any manner they wish one INDIVIDUAL to represent their interests in a decision-making GROUP on the first Level of a CONSOCRATIC government.

5.3.1.2. Each REPRESENTATIVE of a SITE voluntarily gathers together with REPRESENTATIVES from other adjacent SITES into a single 1st LEVEL or NEIGHBOURHOOD GROUP of a size that allows that NEIGHBOURHOOD

GROUP to reach all its decisions by consensus as well as comply with the GROUP size limits set out in Part 5.4 below

5.3.1.3. Each NEIGHBOURHOOD GROUP then selects by CONSENSUS one REPRESENTATIVE from among its MEMBERS to represent that GROUP'S interests in a second LEVEL of government, or VILLAGE GROUP.

5.3.1.4. Each new VILLAGE GROUP formed shall be of a size that allows all its MEMBERS to reach decisions by consensus and comply with the GROUP size limits set out in Part 5.4. below.

5.3.1.5. The MEMBERS of each VILAGE GROUP then select by CONSENSUS one REPRESENTATIVE from among its MEMBERS to represent their interests in a yet higher third LEVEL GROUP or TOWN GROUP,

5.3.1.6. Additional LEVELS of GROUPS (CITY, REGION, STATE, ETC.) are formed in a like manner as needed until the TOPMOST LEVEL contains only one GROUP.

5.4. Size of a Group

5.4.1. The minimum number of MEMBERS in any GROUP is six.

5.4.2. The maximum number of MEMBERS in any GROUP is 42, although the maximum practical GROUP size is 30 members. This is because each GROUP shall comply with Parts 5.4.4 and 5.4.5 below.

5.4.3. The optimum number of representatives in all groups is best kept between eleven and twenty one.

5.4.4. Every MEMBER in a single GROUP shall be able to sit side by side in a single circle one MEMBER deep so that every MEMBER of that GROUP is clearly visible to all other MEMBERS of that GROUP all of the time.

5.4.5. Every MEMBER in a GROUP shall be able to be heard by all other MEMBERS of that GROUP without the use of

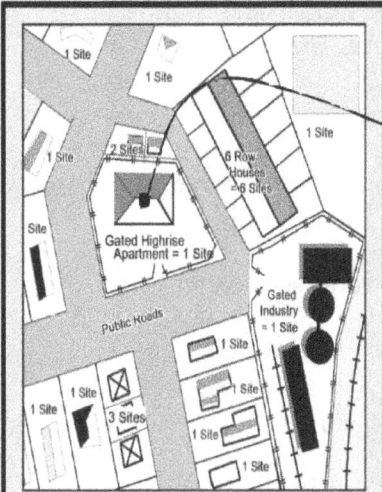

Typical "Sites" in
Structured Consensus Decision-Making

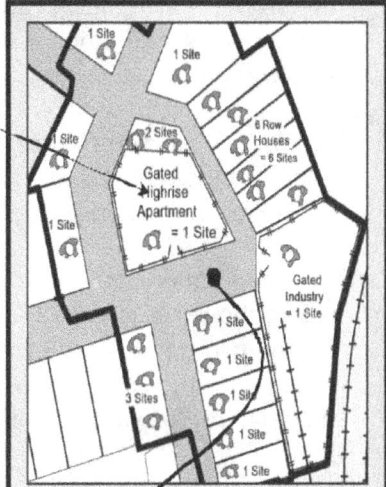

A Typical Level 1 "Neighborhood" Group
in Structured Consensus Decision-Making

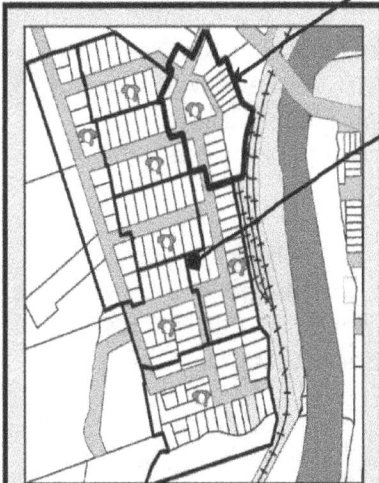

A Typical Level 2 "Village" Group with
Representatives from 8 Neighborhood Groups

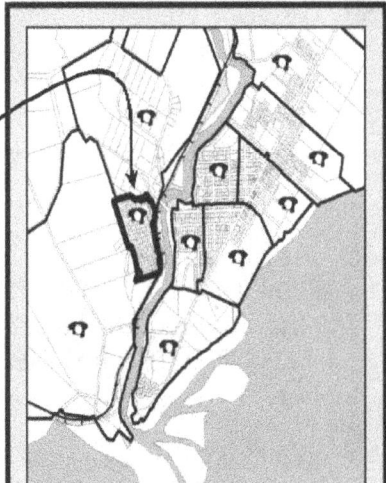

A Typical Level 3 "Town" Group with
Representatives from 10 Village Groups

electronic hearing aids, radios, loudspeakers and other techniques for enhancing sound. The only two exceptions of this are that:

5.4.5.1. Any or all members of a group may use electronic hearing aids to discretely improve poor hearing and to allow access to translation services, and,

5.4.5.2. All members may use electronic screens with microphones and speakers to see and hear everyone in the group, provided that all members are shown together in real time on a single screen, each person with a similar sized head facing forward, and the group contains 36 members or less.

5.4.6. IF any GROUP MEMBERSHIP falls below the permitted minimum size of 6 MEMBERS, it shall disband

5.5. Functions of a Group:

5.5.1. GROUPS are responsible for all decision-making within a CONSOCRACY, apart from personal decisions made by an INDIVIDUAL and internal decisions made within any SITE, HOUSEHOLD, ASSOCIATION, ENTERPRISE or INSTITUTION unless they choose to become a SUB-GROUP.

5.5.2. Any human initiated or aided CHANGE that may AFFECT the ENVIRONMENT outside the SITE on which it occurs shall require the permission of the GROUP responsible for all AFFECTED PARTIES prior to that CHANGE taking place.

5.5.3. The GROUP responsible for all AFFECTED PARTIES may permit, permit with CONDITIONS or prohibit any EFFECT of the proposed CHANGE.

5.5.4. If any CONDITION imposed by a GROUP in consideration

of an EFFECT beyond the site on which it occurs, cannot be met by those responsible for the EFFECT, the CHANGE is prohibited.

5.5.5. Every human initiated or aided CHANGE which AFFECTS the ENVIRONMENT outside the SITE on which it occurs and which has not been permitted by the GROUP responsible for all AFFECTED PARTIES may be immediately stopped and removed by that GROUP and the environment reinstated by any peaceful, environmentally sensitive means, and those INDIVIDUALS responsible for the CHANGE may be fined, confined and/or otherwise brought to social responsibility by that GROUP, where reasonable, at the expense of the GROUP which created the change.

5.6. Sub-Groups

5.6.1. A SUB-GROUP is an ASSOCIATION, ENTERPRISE OR INSTITUTION which chooses to follow the same GROUP decision-making structure and procedures set out in Parts 5.7 and 5.8 below, with the following additional provisions:

5.6.1.1. SUB-GROUPS may be formed on any single LEVEL of a CONSOCRACY with the CONSENSUS of the GLx GROUP at that LEVEL, ("x" being the number of the LEVEL)

5.6.1.2. Every SUB-GROUP shall be identified by the prefix GLxSy ("x" being the number of the LEVEL and "y" being the name of the SUB-GROUP)

5.6.1.3. Every SUB-GROUP shall provide one of its MEMBERS to LINK the GLxSy SUB-GROUP'S interest in the GLx GROUP meetings and to LINK the interests of the GLx GROUP in GLxSy SUB-GROUP meetings unless it is LINKED by shared membership through another SUB-GROUP to the GLx GROUP

5.6.1.4. The number of SUB-GROUPS permitted to LINK directly to a GLx LEVEL Group is limited by the NUMBER of other

MEMBERS that are permitted in that LEVEL GROUP in compliance with Part 5.4 above

5.6.1.5. SUB-GROUPS may be LINKED through a shared MEMBER to other SUB-GROUPS which do not have direct access to the GLx GROUP at that LEVEL

5.7. Group Decision-Making:

5.7.1. All GROUP decisions shall be made by the CONSENSUS of its MEMBERS.

5.7.2. There shall be no obligation to take a formal vote of MEMBERS for any GROUP to reach any decision, although this may occur at the CHAIRPERSON'S discretion.

5.7.3. A GROUP decision occurs at the point when no MEMBER of the GROUP opposes a proposed CHANGE. No GROUP decision shall be reached until this occurs.

5.7.4. All decision-making is undertaken by the lowest LEVEL GROUP able to fully represent the interests of those INDIVIDUALS and the ENVIRONMENT AFFECTED by an existing or proposed CHANGE

5.7.5. The purpose of any GROUP decision is to manage CHANGE in a way that:

5.7.5.1. Allows and encourages humankind to achieve the GOALS of HUMANITY set out in Part 3. and

5.7.5.2. Upholds and enforces the RIGHTS AND RESPONSI-BILITIES of INDIVIDUALS and GROUPS set out in Part 4, as they may be legally amended and applied from time to time, and

5.7.5.3. Complies with the RULES and REGULATIONS set out in Parts 5 and 6, as they may be legally amended and applied from time to time.

And in a manner which:

5.7.5.4 Avoids any CHANGE to the ENVIRONMENT outside the SITE on which it occurs, or

5.7.5.5. Where the CHANGE to the ENVIRONMENT outside the SITE on which it occurs can be made acceptable to the GROUP(S) AFFECTED, remedies any detrimental EFFECT of any CHANGE to the ENVIRONMENT outside the SITE on which it occurs, or

5.7.5.6. Where this is not practicable but the detrimental EFFECT(S) can be made acceptable to the GROUP(S) AFFECTED, minimizes the detrimental EFFECT(S) of any CHANGE to the ENVIRONMENT and compensates those AFFECTED for any detrimental EFFECT that is incurred, to the satisfaction of all GROUP MEMBERS.

5.7.6. Each MEMBER of a GROUP, other than that GROUP'S REPRESENTATIVE, shall, by the CONSENSUS of all MEMBERS, be given responsibility for advocating one of the five sets of SYSTEMS identified in Part 5.8, below.

5.7.7. The number of MEMBERS in a GROUP responsible for advocating each of the five SYSTEMS identified in Part 5.8 below shall be as equal as possible, with not more than one MEMBER difference between all 5 sets of SYSTEMS.

5.7.8. Where there are more than the minimum number of MEMBERS in a GROUP, those MEMBERS in excess of the minimum (other than that GROUP'S REPRESENTATIVE) may be given additional specialist responsibility for advocating one or more subsets within their given set of SYSTEMS with the CONSENSUS of the other MEMBERS of the GROUP.

5.7.9. No GROUP shall reach a decision unless:

5.7.9.1. The REPRESENTATIVE of that GROUP is present, and

5.7.9.2. At least 80% of that GROUP's MEMBERS are present, and

5.7.9.3. At least 5 MEMBERS of that GROUP are present who are not on probation (see Part 5.7.12 below) and who have each been given responsibility for advocating a different one of the five sets of SYSTEMS described in 5.8 below.

5.7.10. No absent MEMBER of a GROUP may participate in that GROUP'S decision-making, without the prior CONSESUS of that GROUP'S MEMBERS.

5.7.11. Prior to any GROUP decision, Each MEMBER shall identify for all other MEMBERS of that GROUP, the potential EFFECTS of the decision on those SYSTEMS and SYSTEM subsets identified in Part 5.8 that are under his or her responsibility as far as he or she is able, with or without the help of professional assistance.

5.7.12. Every new MEMBER of a GROUP shall be a PROBATIONARY MEMBER and may not block a decision made by his or her new GROUP until the new MEMBER has participated in at least six of that GROUP'S meetings, unless this provision is waived by all other MEMBERS of that GROUP.

5.7.13. Any MEMBER of a GROUP may be removed immediately by the CONSENSUS of all other GROUP MEMBERS for intentional wrongdoing, which may include deliberately not upholding the GOALS, PRINCIPLES, RIGHTS, RESPONSIBILITIES and RULES of this PLAN or participating in decision-making with an undisclosed CONFLICT OF INEREST in the matter at hand.

5.8. The Five Sets of Systems

5.8.1. PERSONAL SYSTEMS are those SYSTEMS of CHANGE that are unique to an individual and arise from the actions of a person's own body, mind, character, experience and response to the environment around him or her. Such SYSTEMS include those involving the consumption of food, the occupation of shelter, the establishment and maintenance of friendships, the procreation and nurturing of children, the ownership of physical and intellectual property, the pursuit of pleasure and happiness, the feeling and expression of emotions, and the perception of the five bodily senses. By definition, however, they exclude ECONOMIC and EQUITY SYSTEMS.

5.8.2. ECONOMIC SYSTEMS are those SYSTEMS of CHANGE that involve the private transfer of RESOURCES between SYSTEMS. The private transfer of RESOURCES can occur through RESOURCE use, work or other form of exchange and is identified by a CHANGE in ownership or value. Such activities as banking, administration, professional services, personal services, trade, industry, construction, mining and commercial agriculture are all ECONOMIC SYSTEMS.

5.8.3. EQUITY SYSTEMS are those SYSTEMS of CHANGE designed to ensure fairness, impartiality and justice. The term is not a reference to the residual value of encumbered property, the term's other meaning. They are SYSTEMS whose primary purpose is to maintain independent public control over the relationships that other SYSTEMS have with each other. They include our political SYSTEMS, tax systems, PLANNING & evaluation SYSTEMS, weights and measures systems, defense SYSTEMS, police SYSTEMS, legal SYSTEMS, punishment SYSTEMS and public records SYSTEMS.

5.8.4. COMMUNITY SYSTEMS are those SYSTEMS of CHANGE that involve collective human responses to the ENVIRONMENT. In general, they are larger public versions of PERSONAL SYSTEMS but by definition do not include either ECONOMIC or EQUITY SYSTEMS. COMMUNITY SYSTEMS include public media SYSTEMS, public health SYSTEMS, public education SYSTEMS, religious SYSTEMS, cultural heritage SYSTEMS, public recreation SYSTEMS, and social support SYSTEMS like disability and unemployment benefits, public housing, health insurance and retirement schemes.

5.8.5. ENVIRONMENTAL SYSTEMS are those SYSTEMS of CHANGE that provide the physical setting that allows each of us to exist. They are essentially the various "eco" systems found on our globe, whether or not they contain humans or have been modified by them. They include all SYSTEMS involving natural RESOURCES such as land, water, minerals, air, plants and animals (including humans), plus all movement SYSTEMS and SYSTEMS involving physical or technological improvements added by humans such as buildings and roads (i.e. the physical attributes of civilization).

5.9. Group Meetings:

5.9.1. A GROUP meeting may be called at any time by the CHAIRPERSON, by the ARBITER or by any three MEMBERS of the GROUP provided that all GROUP MEMBERS are notified of the GROUP meeting in compliance with Part 5.9.2, 5.9.3 & 5.9.4 below.

5.9.2. Notice of every GROUP meeting date, time and previously agreed location, along with an agenda of the topics to be covered and where relevant, all background information and prepared reports, shall be sent to all MEMBERS of that GROUP, delivered either;

5.9.2.1. Directly by hand to the MEMBER, or

5.9.2.2. By posting it to the MEMBER at their address of record, or

5.9.2.3. By facsimile to the facsimile telephone number of record of the MEMBER, or

5.9.2.4. By electronic message to the "E-Mail" address of record of the MEMBER, or

5.9.2.5. By any other method agreed at a previous GROUP meeting.

5.9.3. Notice of a GROUP meeting together with all relevant background information and reports shall reach every GROUP MEMBER'S HOUSEHOLD not less than seven days prior to a LEVEL 1 or 2 GROUP (GL1 & GL2) meeting , 14 days prior to a LEVEL 3 or 4 GROUP (GL3 & GL4) meeting, and 28 days prior to any GROUP meeting above LEVEL 4.

5.9.4. Where the CHAIRPERSON determines that a GROUP meeting is urgent for any reason, or where an ARBITER determines that a GROUP meeting is urgent to ensure justice, he or she may include a statement to that effect and the reasons why in the notice of meeting, and reduce the required period of notification for such meeting to any "urgent notification" period previously agreed by that GROUP.

5.9.5. Only matters identified in the notice of meeting may be raised, discussed and decided upon in a GROUP meeting.

5.9.6. Meetings may be held either:

5.9.6.1. By assembling all MEMBERS of the GROUP together at the place, date and time authorized by the CHAIRPERSON for the GROUP meeting, or

5.9.6.2. By means of audio and visual communication by which all MEMBERS of the GROUP may simultaneously hear and see each other facing forward with a similar head size on a single screen throughout the meeting, or

5.9.6.3. By use of written and/or graphically descriptive resolutions sent to all MEMBERS and returned with the written response of each MEMBER to the CHAIRPERSON. Any such resolution may consist of several documents in like form, signed or otherwise formally authorised by one or more MEMBERS. Where there is reasonable confidence in the authenticity of the transmissions, facsimile, 'E-mail', and other methods of information exchange may be used, or

5.9.6.4. By use of computer aided methods such as Loomio, Lectica and Value Knowledge Management, or

5.9.6.5. By any other method agreed by the CONSENSUS of the GROUP.

5.9.7. GROUP meetings may be run in any manner considered appropriate by the CHAIRPERSON, and apart from the requirement that all decisions must be reached by the CONSENSUS of all MEMBERS and all decision are recorded by the GROUP PUBLICIST, may utilize any parliamentary procedure, committee rules, the Delphi Technique, computer assisted "Value Knowledge Management" systems or other decision-making methodology.

5.9.8. Every GROUP decision shall be recorded by the GROUP'S PUBLICIST immediately after it is reached and then read back to the GROUP in attendance immediately. No decision shall take effect until all MEMBERS in attendance have heard it read or otherwise clearly indicate his or her non-opposition to it.

5.9.9. Proceedings of GROUP meetings shall be electronically recorded in a manner that allows the proceedings to be put on-line and will allow them to be transcribed to hard copy at a later date if required, and shall be held in perpetuity by the PUBLICIST of the GROUP or by the GROUP'S administration.

5.10. Resolving Disagreements in Decision-Making

5.10.1. When CONSENSES among GROUP MEMBERS cannot be reached on a proposed CHANGE or on an existing but unapproved CHANGE, then on the direction of the CHAIRPERSON the GROUP shall seek assistance, including:

5.10.1.1. Using a MEDIATOR, or

5.10.1.2. Using the Delphi Technique, or

5.10.1.3. Using Value Knowledge Management, Loomio or other computerized decision-making assistance, or

5.10.1.4. Using any alternative method of reaching a decision previously agreed by that GROUP, such as CONSENSUS less one, or majority vote DECISION-MAKING,

5.10.2. If reaching a GROUP decision with assistance is not successful then the full context of the decision impasse, including the specific differences of opinion and the reasons for them, shall be set down in writing by those on all sides of the issue.

5.10.3. Once the description of the issues surrounding the CHANGE are confirmed by the CONSENSUS of the GROUP, the REPRESENTATIVE of that GROUP shall then take that written statement to the GROUP in which he or she sits as a MEMBER for resolution.

5.10.4. The GROUP that is asked to resolve the decision-making impasse of another GROUP may use any resources available to it to reach its decision, which shall be final. If it is unable to reach a decision by consensus, it shall formulate its impasse in the same way set out in Part 5.10.2 and 5.10.3 and refer it along with all original material to another GROUP through its REPRESENTATIVE.

5.10.5. Once a decision of a GROUP has been made, it may not be reconsidered for one year, unless directed to do so by another GROUP through the original GROUP'S REPRESENTATIVE, or unless not to do so would put human life or environmental sustainability at risk and all GROUP MEMBERS agree to reconsider the matter.

5.10.6. After one year, or earlier in the circumstances described in part 5.10.5 above, a GROUP may reconsider any decision it has made previously for any reason, but in doing so, shall take into consideration all events that have occurred since the original decision, and where a party has acted on the basis of the first decision and is detrimentally affected by the second, that GROUP shall compensate that party for all extra costs incurred to comply with the second decision.

5.10.7. As an alternative to granting compensation for a CHANGE to an earlier GROUP decision, the affected party may be granted a special exemption by the GROUP and allowed to continue for a set period or for an indefinite period.

5.11. Delegation of Responsibility

5.11.1. Decision-making responsibilities of a GROUP may be delegated to one or more consenting GROUPS or SUB-GROUPS on any LEVEL with more intimate knowledge of the INDIVIDUALS or ENVIRONMENT involved. However, this is not mandatory.

5.11.2. A GROUP may temporarily delegate any of its decision-making responsibilities at any time to any other consenting GROUP, INSTITUTION, ASSOCIATION, ENTERPRISE or INDIVIDUAL.

5.12. Conflicts of Interest

5.12.1. Any MEMBER who has a CONFLICT OF INTEREST in any matter being considered by a GROUP shall declare that interest to all other MEMBERS of his or her GROUP as soon as it becomes known.

5.12.2. At the discretion of the other MEMBERS, the MEMBER with a CONFLICT OF INTEREST shall abstain from participating in any related discussion or decision on the matter except to respond to questions asked directly by another MEMBER.

5.12.3. Failure to declare a CONFLICT OF INTEREST may, at the discretion of the other MEMBERS of the GROUP, by consensus censure, restrict or terminate his or her MEMBERSHIP in the GROUP.

5.12.4. Any INDIVIDUAL, HOUSEHOLD, AFFILIATION, ASSOCIATION, ENTERPRISE or INSTITUTION may initiate discussions with any GROUP'S LOBBYIST at any time on any matter without creating a conflict of interest for the LOBBYIST or contact initiator. However, no INDIVIDUAL, HOUSEHOLD, AFFILIATION, ASSOCIATION, ENTERPRISE or INSTITUTION may discuss any matter with any other MEMBER of that GROUP if that matter may be discussed at any meeting of that GROUP.

5.13. Group Restructuring and Dissolution

5.13.1. A MEMBER of a GROUP may leave the GROUP and join (subject to Part 5.4 above) any other GROUP on the same LEVEL of his or her choosing at any time. However, when this leaves a GROUP with less than 5 MEMBERS, (excluding that GROUP'S REPRESENTATIVE), sufficient replacement MEMBERS from the same LEVEL shall join that GROUP to meet the minimum number, or those MEMBERS remaining in the GROUP must disband and then may individually join other existing GROUP(S) on the same LEVEL (subject to Part 5.4).

5.13.2. If any GROUP splits apart and creates one or more new GROUPS, the new GROUPS shall each have at least 6 MEMBERS (5 members plus their REPRESENTATIVE) in them initially, and each new GROUP may then select its own REPRESENTATIVE for a GROUP on the next LEVEL provided that the original GROUP contains not less than six MEMBERS (5 members plus their REPRESENTATIVE) or it must be disbanded as per part 5.13.1 above.

5.14. Group Leadership Roles

5.14.1. Every GROUP is required by the CONSENSUS of its MEMBERS to give LEADERSHIP ROLES to all its MEMBERS.

5.14.2. The LEADERSHIP ROLES required in every GROUP (see

also diagram on page 391 below) are:

5.14.2.1.   CHAIRPERSON
5.14.2.2.   PUBLICIST,
5.14.2.3.   ENVIRONMENTALIST.
5.14.2.4.   ECONOMIST,
5.14.2.5.   PUBLIC EMPLOYER,
5.14.2.6.   LOBBYIST,
5.14.2.7.   OMBUDSIST
5.14.2.8.   ARBITER,
5.14.2.9.   CHIEF OFFICER.
5.14.2.10.   ALTERNATE REPRESENTATIVE
5.14.2.11.   REPRESENTATIVE

5.14.3. Those MEMBERS given responsibility for PERSONAL SYSTEMS may be given the LEADERSHIP ROLE of CHAIRPERSON or OMBUDSIST, or both if the GROUP contains less than 11 MEMBERS.

5.14.4. Those MEMBERS given responsibility for ECONOMIC SYSTEMS may be given the LEADERSHIP ROLE of ECONOMIST or LOBBYIST or both if the GROUP contains less than 11 MEMBERS.

5.14.5. Those MEMBERS given responsibility for EQUITY SYSTEMS may be given the LEADERSHIP ROLE of ARBITER or CHIEF OFFICER or both if the GROUP contains less than 11 MEMBERS.

5.14.6. Those MEMBERS given responsibility for COMMUNITY SYSTEMS may be given the LEADERSHIP ROLE of PUBLICIST or PUBLIC EMPLOYER, or both if the GROUP contains less than 11 MEMBERS.

5.14.7. Those MEMBERS given responsibility for ENVIRONMENTAL SYSTEMS may be given the

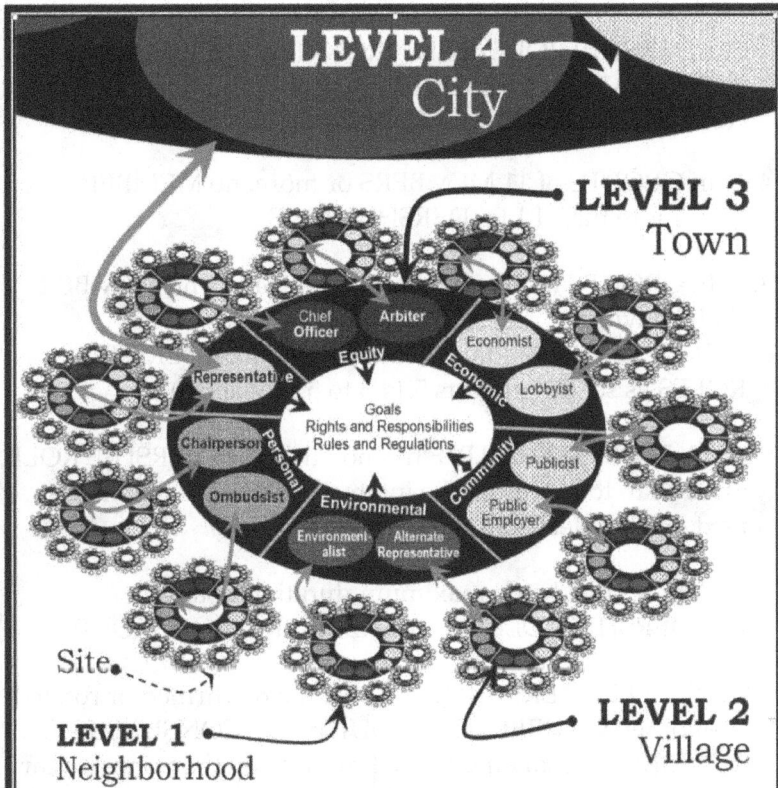

LEVEL 4
City

LEVEL 3
Town

Chief Officer — Arbiter
Equity — Economist
Representative — Economic
Goals
Rights and Responsibilities
Rules and Regulations
Chairperson — Personal — Lobbyist
Ombudsist — Publicist
Environmental — Community
Environment-alist — Alternate Representative — Public Employer

Site

LEVEL 1
Neighborhood

LEVEL 2
Village

First 4 Levels of Structured Consensus Decision-Making In a Consocracy

1. Each black circle represents a single group of representatives.
2. All grey arrows represent a single individual linking together two groups on different levels.
3. All groups on all levels work the same way.

71

LEADERSHIP ROLE of ENVIRONMENTALIST or ALTERNATE REPRESENTATIVE, or both if the GROUP contains less than 11 MEMBERS.

5.14.8. In GROUPS of 11 MEMBERS or more, no MEMBER may have more than 1 LEADERSHIP ROLE

5.14.9. In GROUPS with less than 11 MEMBERS, no MEMBER shall be without a LEADERSHIP ROLE. However MEMBERS may hold up to two related LEADERSHIP ROLES as set out in Parts 5.14.3 to 5.14.7 above.

5.14.10. A REPRESENTATIVE has no other LEADERSHIP ROLE other than to represent the interests of the GROUP in the next level of decision-making.

5.14.11. There shall be no maximum duration of any LEADERSHIP ROLE for any MEMBER in any GROUP.

5.14.12. Each LEADERSHIP ROLE shall be reaffirmed or rotated to another MEMBER of a GROUP by the CONSENSUS of all MEMBERS of that GROUP not more often than once a year and not less often than once every three years.

5.14.13. With the exception of the REPRESENTATIVE position, any vacancy in any LEADERSHIP ROLE listed in Part 5.14.2 above shall be filled by the CONSENSUS of the GROUP as soon as practicable.

5.14.14. A permanently vacant REPRESENTATIVE position shall be automatically filled immediately by the ALTERNATE REPRESENTATIVE.

5.14.15. Each MEMBER may also be given responsibility for such other matters as may be agreed by him or her from time to time with the consensus of his or her GROUP including providing a LINK between a GLx GROUP and any GLxSy

SUB-GROUP, PUBLIC UTILITY, FACILITY or SERVICE not specifically assigned to another MEMBER.

5.14.16. No MEMBER shall have a financial interest in, or be a member of, any privately owned UTILITY, FACILITY OR SERVICE in the area under his or her GROUP'S responsibility if there is a publicly owned UTILITY, FACILITY OR SERVICE available to him or her in that area.

5.14.17. Every MEMBER of a GROUP shall provide his or her full name and personal details for inclusion on a publicly available REGISTER OF PUBIC SERVANTS (See also part 5.29).

5.15. Representative Responsibilities

5.15.1. A REPRESENTATIVE'S primary responsibility is to provide a LINK that allows information to be freely exchanged between any two GROUPS on adjacent LEVELS or on the same LEVEL; the two GROUPS being:

5.15.1.1. The GROUP that selected him or her to represent their interests in a second GROUP and

5.15.1.2. The second GROUP the REPRESENTATIVE joined.

5.15.2. Every GLx GROUP except the TOPMOST GROUP shall select by CONSENSUS a REPRESENTATIVE from its MEMBERS to represent its interests in any GROUP on the next LEVEL. (GLx+1)

5.15.3. The TOPMOST GROUP shall select by CONSENSUS a REPRESENTATIVE to be the HEAD of STATE. This is a figurative position with no individual responsibility other than to represent the interests of the TOPMOST GROUP.

5.15.4. Every GLxSy GROUP shall select by CONSENSUS a REPRESENTATIVE from its MEMBERS to represent its interests in any GLx GROUP or GLxSy SUB-GROUP on the same LEVEL.

5.15.5. No GLx GROUP REPRESENTATIVE may be refused MEMBERSHIP in any GROUP on the next LEVEL. (GLx+1) even if the GROUP to be joined has the maximum permitted number of MEMBERS (If it does, the GROUP being joined may have to split into two or more GROUPS), unless:

5.15.5.1. The GLx GROUP REPRESENTATIVE seeking to become a MEMBER in a GLx +1 GROUP does not represent the minimum number of INDIVIDUALS for that LEVEL of GROUP as set out in 19.5.15.8 below, or

5.15.5.2. The GLx GROUP REPRESENTATIVE seeking to become a MEMBER in a GROUP on LEVELS 1, 2 or 3 does not represent a SITE that is adjacent to, or across a PUBLIC PATH, public park or other public facility from another SITE represented by a MEMBER of that GROUP.

5.15.6. A REPRESENTATIVE shall participate only in the highest two GROUP LEVELS (GLx and GLx+1) of decision-making for which he or she has been selected.

5.15.7. When a GROUP'S REPRESENTATIVE joins a second LEVEL GROUP he or she looses the title of REPRESENTATIVE in that second LEVEL GROUP and becomes just a MEMBER of that GROUP. If that MEMBER is then selected by that second LEVEL GROUP to represent its interest in a third LEVEL GROUP, his or her association with the first LEVEL GROUP as its REPRESENTATIVE is automatically terminated and the vacant REPRESENTATIVE position in the first LEVEL GROUP shall be immediately filled by the first GROUP"S ALTERNATE REPRESENTATIVE

5.15.8. The minimum number of SITES and INDIVIDUALS represented by a REPRESENTATIVE is as follows:

Individual/Household (site)	1 site	(1 person)
Level 1 Group (Neighborhood)	10 sites	(10 people)
Level 2 Group (Village)	100 sites	(100 people)
Level 3 Group (Town)	1,000 sites	(1,000 people)
Level 4 Group (City)	10,000 sites	(10,000 people)
Level 5 Group (Region)	100,000 sites	(100,000 people)
Level 6 Group (State)	1,000,000 sites	(1,000,000 people)
Level 7 Group (Country)	10,000,000 sites	(10,000,000 people)
Level 8 Group (Continent)	100,000,000 sites	(100,000,000 people)
Level 9 Group (World)	1,000,000,000 sites	(1,000,000,000 people)

5.15.9.CHAIRPERSON Responsibilities:

5.15.9.1. In addition to those leadership role responsibilities listed in 5.14 above, the responsibilities of the CHAIRPERSON shall include calling a meeting (or an urgent meeting) of the GROUP for any reason in accordance with 5.9 above, and

5.15.9.2. Coordinating, mediating and running GROUP meetings, and

5.15.9.3. with the CONSENSUS of the GROUP, setting the operating procedures and rules of that GROUP, and

5.15.9.4. Coordinating with the CONSENSUS of the GROUP the selection of GROUP MEMBERS to fill all required LEADRSHIP ROLES of the GROUP.

5.15.10. PUBLICIST Responsibilities;

5.15.10.1. In addition to those LEADERSHIP ROLE responsibilities listed in 5.14 above, the responsibilities of the PUBLICIST shall include recording the proceedings of GROUP meetings and the decisions reached, and

5.15.10.2. Receiving, organizing and distributing information relevant to GROUP decision-making, and

5.15.10.3. Reporting GROUP ACTIVITIES and decisions to the PUBLIC MEDIA,

5.15.11.   ENVIRONMENTALIST Responsibilities;

5.15.11.1. In addition to those LEADERSHIP ROLE responsibilities listed in 5.14 above, the ENVIRONMENTALIST shall provide PLANNING and RESOURCE management advice to the GROUP, including the physical infrastructure of education and healthcare facilities and the network of PUBLIC PATHS.

5.15.12.   ECONOMIST Responsibilities;

5.15.12.1. In addition to those LEADERSHIP ROLE responsibilities listed in 5.14 above, the responsibilities of the ECONOMIST shall include Providing MARKET PLACE advice to the GROUP, and,

5.15.12.2. Providing taxation and business advice to the GROUP,

5.15.13.   PUBLIC EMPLOYER Responsibilities;

5.15.13.1. In addition to those LEADERSHIP ROLE responsibilities listed in 5.14 above, the PUBLIC EMPLOYER is responsible for the operational management of education and healthcare facilities and the roading network, and has the authority to employ any one out of work in the public sector at a LIVING WAGE and can modify any terms of employment to suit the particular interests, skills, age, and abilities of that INDIVIDUAL (where this service exists),

5.15.14.   LOBBYIST Responsibilities;

5.15.14.1. In addition to those LEADERSHIP ROLE responsibilities listed in 5.14 above, the responsibilities of the LOBBYIST shall include the conveyance of information, view or opinion received from an INDIVIDUAL,

HOUSEHOLD, AFFILIATION, ASSOCIATION, ENTERPRISE, or INSTITUTION to other MEMBERS of his or her GROUP,

5.15.15. OMBUDSIST Responsibilities;

5.15.15.1. In addition to those LEADERSHIP ROLE responsibilities listed in 5.14 above, the responsibilities of the OMBUDSIST shall include the right to review any decision made by a lower LEVEL GROUP that is represented by a MEMBER of the OMBUDSIST'S GROUP, following the direct request of a MEMBER of that lower LEVEL GROUP, and the right to choose not to review any decision for any reason, and

5.15.15.2. The right to access all information available to any MEMBER of the GROUP that originally made the decision being reviewed, and

5.15.15.3. The right to attend any meeting or interview any MEMBER of the GROUP whose decision is being reviewed, although he or she shall not have the right to participate in that GROUP, and

5.15.15.4. The right upon review of any decision under his or her investigation, to either:

> 5.15.15.4.1. Publicize the results of his or her review of the GROUP'S original decision in any manner he or she chooses, or

> 5.15.15.4.2. Drop the matter from any further consideration with or without an explanation.

5.15.15.5. The Ombudsist alone may not force a lower level group to change its decision, but the Ombudsist's group, by consensus, may require a decision to be reconsidered by a higher level group if the likely effects of the lower level group's decision went beyond its jurisdiction.

5.15.16. ARBITER Responsibilities;

5.15.16.1. In addition to those LEADERSHIP ROLE responsibilities listed in 5.14 above, the responsibilities of the ARBITER shall include providing GROUP liaison with the activities of a COURT, and

5.15.16.2. Directly liaising with any CHIEF OFFICER, and

5.15.16.3. Calling an urgent meeting of the GROUP to enable justice, and

5.15.16.4. Recommending to GROUP MEMBER'S their response to any breach of a RIGHT, RESPONSIBILITY, RULE, or REGULATION, or any resolution to a dispute.

5.15.17. CHIEF OFFICER Responsibilities

5.15.17.1. In addition to those LEADERSHIP ROLE responsibilities listed in 5.14 above, the responsibilities of the CHIEF OFFICER shall include providing Group liaison with its Internal Police Force, and

5.15.17.2. Providing Group liaison with any Emergency or Fire Service,

5.15.17.3. Directly liaising with any ARBITER,

5.15.17.4. Responding to all requests of a COURT,

5.15.18. ALTERNATE REPRESENTATIVE Responsibilities:

5.15.18.1. In addition to those LEADERSHIP ROLE responsibilities listed in Part 5.14 above, an ALTERNATE REPRESENTATIVE'S primary responsibility is to remain knowledgeable of the activities of the GROUP'S REPRESENTATIVE so that he or she may be able to fulfill at short notice the REPRESENTATIVE'S role of LINK to the next GROUP LEVEL (GLx+1) either temporarily or permanently.

5.15.18.2. Other responsibilities of an ALTERNATE REPRESENTATIVE include taking responsibility for one of the five sets of SYSTEMS identified in 19.5.8 above and such other matters as may be agreed by him or her from time to time with the consensus of his or her GROUP, including providing a LINK between a GLx GROUP and any GLxSy SUB-GROUP, PUBLIC UTILITY, FACILITY or SERVICE not specifically assigned to another MEMBER.

5.15.18.3. After a GROUP selects a REPRESENTATIVE from its own MEMBERS to represent its interests in another GROUP, it shall also select by CONSENSUS another MEMBER who is not the same sex as the REPRESENTATIVE, to be the ALTERNATE REPRESENTATIVE and represent its interests in that same GROUP in the event that the REPRESENTATIVE is unable to attend to his or her responsibilities for any reason.

5.15.18.4. An ALTERNATE REPRESENTATIVE may take responsibility for any matter delegated to him or her by the GROUP including providing GROUP liaison on any PUBLIC UTILITY, FACILITY or SERVICE not specifically assigned to another MEMBER.

5.15.18.5. In the event of an illness or other temporary absence of the REPRESENTATIVE, the ALTERNATE REPRESENTATIVE shall attend to all responsibilities of the REPRESENTATIVE.

5.15.18.6. If a REPRESENTATIVE dies, resigns or has been selected to represent the interests of his or her new GROUP in yet another GROUP (usually on a higher LEVEL) then the ALTERNATE REPRESENTATIVE shall immediately fill the position of the REPRESENTATIVE and a new ALTERNATE REPRESENTATIVE selected.

5.16. SITE Status and Functions:

5.16.1. A SITE is any SPACE or collection of contiguous SPACES which is entirely under the control of an identifiable owner or occupier. It includes PUBLIC LAND and PRIVATE LAND whose boundaries are recorded in public records, or whose boundaries are reasonably distinguishable by natural or physical changes in landscape, material composition, surface texture or other obvious visual feature that can be used to define ownership or occupancy.

5.16.2. Every SITE shall be directly accessible to all members of the public from a PUBLIC PATH all of the time.

5.16.3. A SITE may involve SPACE not at ground level such as a room or collection of rooms in a BUILDING and it may involve distinguishable portions of water areas, such as harbors and flood plains.

5.16.4. Any SITE described in public records in only two dimensions, such as land ownership titles, shall be deemed to contain a third, vertical dimension which as a minimum includes all existing STRUCTURES situated on that two dimensional SPACE, and in addition extends not less than 10 metres below and not less than 10 metres above ground level unless a greater or lesser interpretation is clearly obvious by a STRUCTURE within the SPACE. It includes any single SPACE occupied by a HOUSEHOLD, ASSOCIATION, ENTERPRISE or INSTITUTION.

5.16.5. Every SITE shall be subject to the RULES of this PLAN if an ACTIVITY on that SITE AFFECTS the ENVIRONMENT outside that SITE. If this occurs, it shall be subject to all decisions reached by any GROUP representing that SITE.

5.16.6. Every SITE shall be represented in a LEVEL 1 or Neighbourhood GROUP by not more than one INDIVIDUAL.

5.16.7. HOUSEHOLDS occupying a single SITE may use any method to select the INDIVIDUAL that represents its interests in a GL1 GROUP.

5.16.8. All SITES that do not contain a HOUSEHOLD may be represented by any INDIVIDUAL not associated with or representing another SITE.

5.15.9 SITES that do not contain a HOUSEHOLD or SITES containing HOUSEHOLDS, all of whom choose not to select an INDIVIDUAL to represent their interests in a GROUP, shall be represented by the closest or most contiguous GROUP to that SITE.

5.17. INDIVIDUALS, HOUSEHOLDS, ASSOCIATIONS, ENTERPRISES and INSTITUTIONS Status and Functions:

5.17.1. INDIVIDUALS, HOUSEHOLDS, ASSOCIATIONS, ENTERPRISES and INSTITUTIONS may make personal or internal decisions in any manner they choose.

5.17.2. Whether or not any formal decision-making organization exists, individually and collectively every INDIVIDUAL, HOUSEHOLD, ASSOCIATION, ENTERPRISE or INSTITUTION shall comply with the RIGHTS AND RESPONSIBILITIES set out in Part 4 of this PLAN.

5.17.3. No ACTIVITY of an INDIVIDUAL, HOUSEHOLD, ASSOCIATION, ENTERPRISE or INSTITUTION shall have or create an EFFECT on the ENVIRONMENT outside the site on which it occurs without the written consent of the GLx GROUP that is responsible for the ENVIRONMENT AFFECTED.

5.17.4. An INDIVIDUAL may not represent the interests of more than one SITE or participate in more than one GROUP on the first (NEIGHBOURHOOD) LEVEL of government.

5.18. Group Administration Status and Functions:

5.18.1. Every GROUP shall have access to professional staff, including private consultants, to provide advice and administrative services to help the GROUP reach and implement its decisions. Such staff includes all members of the GROUP'S COURT and Internal Police.

5.18.2. Advice and administrative services may be provided in the form of one or more SUB-GROUPS LINKED to that GROUP.

5.18.3. The amount of advice and administrative assistance available to a GROUP may vary from GROUP to GROUP depending on the LEVEL of the GROUP, the complexity of possible CHANGES the GROUP must deal with and the potential EFFECTS of the decisions being reached.

5.18.4. Administrative staff available to the GROUP shall be responsible for maintaining computerized cadastral maps, Google Earth maps, hard copy maps or other records which uniquely identify (at a global level) the boundaries of all SITES and undefined areas of land under the responsibility of the GROUP.

5.18.5. Administrative staff available to the GROUP shall be responsible for maintaining hard copy and computerized records containing the name, globally unique IDENTIFICATION CODE, HOUSEHOLD SITE location and contact details of all INDIVIDUALS under the responsibility of the GROUP.

5.18.6. All administrative staff shall provide for public information, his or her full name and personal details for inclusion on the REGISTER OF PUBIC SERVANTS (See also Part 5.19)

5.18.7. No administrative staff included on the REGISTER OF PUBLIC SERVANTS shall have a financial interest in, or be a member of, any privately owned UTILITY, FACILITY OR SERVICE in the area under his or her administration's responsibility if there is a publicly owned UTILITY, FACILITY OR SERVICE available to him or her in that area.

5.18.8. All GROUP MEMBERS and supporting administrative staff on the third LEVEL of a CONSOCRACY and above shall be compensated for their participation in or assistance to a GROUP at an amount commensurate to their responsibilities, with the exception that any INDIVIDUAL employed by an EMPLOYER of a GROUP shall be employed at the LIVING WAGE applicable to the jurisdiction of the GROUP. (See Part 6.19.5)

5.19. Register of Public Servants

5.19.1. A REGISTER OF PUBLIC SERVANTS shall be kept by every GROUP administration. It shall be publicly accessible and kept in both hard copy and on-line electronic format, and include the full names and personal details of all GROUP and SUB-GROUP MEMBERS and employed administrative staff, including all experts and consultants engaged by or for the GROUP or its administration for any reason, as well as all staff of all PUBLIC UTILITIES, FACILITIES and SERVICES,

5.19.2. The personal details required of all GROUP MEMBERS, administrative staff, experts and consultants shall include:

5.19.2.1. All contact details, including legal name, household address, contact telephone/cell phone/email address, etc

5.19.2.2. IF a GROUP MEMBER, the name and location of the GROUP he or she currently represents, the names and locations of all previous GROUPS REPRESENTED and the total number of INDIVIDUALS currently REPRESENTED as accurately as record keeping allows,

5.19.2.3. ID photo not more than 3 years old,

5.19.2.4. Personal educational background,

5.19.2.5. Personal work experience,

5.19.2.6. Personal interests,

5.19.2.7. Personal criminal record if any, and bankruptcy position.

5.19.2.8. Names of all occupants of his or her HOUSEHOLD,

5.19.2.9. Names and contact addresses of all AFFILIATIONS, ASSOCIATIONS, ENTERPRISES and INSTITUTIONS in which the INDIVIDUAL is a member and

5.19.2.10. A personal statement describing why he or she is working for the PUBLIC.

5.20. Identification Codes:

5.20.1. Every INDIVIDUAL shall be issued a globally unique IDENTIFICATION CODE by the TOPMOST GROUP Administration and every INDIVIDUAL who uses any PUBLIC LAND or any public UTILITY, FACILITY OR SERVICE or who engages in GROUP CONSENSUS decision-making shall provide this code to any GROUP Administrative staff if officially requested to do so in writing.

5.20.2. It shall be illegal to disclose, or use for any private or commercial purpose any personal information gathered using the globally unique IDENTIFICATION CODE, with the exception that all GROUPS, including all UTILITIES, FACILITIES and SERVICES within their jurisdiction may internally cross link information on INDIVIDUALS using this code.

Part 6. Other Recommended Rules:

6.1. Status of Part 6:

6.1.1. No RULE in this Part (6) shall take effect until the TOPMOST GROUP adopts it by CONSENSUS.

6.1.2. Once the TOPMOST GROUP adopts a RULE set out in this Part (6), it may not be modified, added to or deleted without the CONSENSUS of the TOPMOST GROUP.

6.1.3. The purposes of the RULES in this Part (6) are to encourage peaceful co-existence between people, achieve social justice and promote environmental sustainability. They are not fundamental to the operation of a CONSOCRACY, but they may significantly improve its operation.

6.1.4. REGULATIONS may be made to clarify or expand upon any RIGHT, RESPONSIBILITY or RULE of this PLAN. They may be made by any GROUP for any reason including clarifying the timing of implementation, the methodology of implementation or any other relevant matter, provided the original meaning of the RIGHT, RESPONSIBILITY or RULE is not altered.

6.2. Taxes

6.2.1. There shall be no tax on INDIVIDUAL or HOUSEHOLD income or on ENTERPRISE profit with the exception that taxes on INDIVIDUAL income or profit may be collected on the earnings of any INDIVIDUAL declared BANKRUPT, as one way to repay any debt owing.

6.2.2. EVERY PUBLIC UTILITY, FACILITY AND SERVICE provided to INDIVIDUALS shall be financed through the imposition of two forms of taxes by the TOPMOST GROUP, namely;

6.2.2.1. RESOURCE USE TAXES or "RUT", which are collected

once or periodically for the handling, use, restoration and/or replacement of any RESOURCE

6.2.2.2. Value Added GOODS AND SERVICES TAXES or "GST", which are applied to the purchase of any tradable commodity, service or intellectual property including any RESOURCE. It is paid by the buyer based on a percentage of the purchase price. However, the seller is only required to pay the collector of the tax a tax on the amount received from the buyer minus the amount paid by the seller to purchase the original raw or wholesale goods or to provide the required services.

6.2.3. Every SITE, and every existing or new ASSOCIATION, ENTERPRISE and INSTITUTION located and/or operating within the area of responsibility of the TOPMOST GROUP shall be issued with a globally unique IDENTIFICATION CODE.

6.2.4. As part of a new tax system, new records shall be created or existing records updated under the direction of the TOPMOST GROUP, and then continuously maintained by the TOPMOST GROUP to clearly identify the globally unique IDENTIFICATION CODE of every INDIVIDUAL, SITE, ASSOCIATION, ENTERPRISE and INSTITUTION within the area of responsibility of the TOPMOST GROUP.

6.2.5. GROUP records shall link the IDENTIFICATION CODES of every SITE, ASSOCIATION, ENTERPRISE and INSTITUTION to the IDENTIFICATION CODES of every INDIVIDUAL that has in interest in them, including owners, directors and employees. (See RIGHTS AND RESPONSIBILTIES 4.14.2 and RULE 5.20)).

6.3. Resource Use Tax (Rut) Collection and Disbursement:

6.3.1. The TOPMOST GROUP shall determine what RESOURCES are taxable and how, when, where and how much RESOURCE USE TAX (RUT) will be collected.

6.3.2. Prior to the establishment of any RESOURCE USE TAX (RUT) on land, RESOURCES, or POLLUTION, new records shall be created or existing records updated to clearly identify who, personally, has ownership rights to every SITE and RESOURCE under the responsibility of the GROUP, including every PUBLIC SITE and RESOURCE.

6.3.3. RESOURCE USE TAXES (RUT) shall be set and collected by the TOPMOST GROUP and redistributed to each LEVEL GROUP under its responsibility in variable amounts in proportion to the services provided by each GROUP.

6.3.4. RUT Taxes on land shall be paid annually by all land owners based on a percentage of the SALEABLE VALUE of the land as if all buildings and structures on the land were removed, with four exceptions:

6.3.4.1. Land that is publicly owned and permanently available for PUBLIC use, such as roads, parks, schools and health care facilities shall not be taxed,

6.3.4.2. Land that is exclusively occupied by a publicly accessible church, church hall, cemetery or memorial garden shall not be taxed,

6.3.4.3. RURAL LAND shall not be taxed. This includes all land this is in, or regenerating to, its natural state,

6.3.4.4. Any URBAN DEVELOPMENT that is not contiguous to an existing COMMUNITY shall be taxed at the average SALEABLE VALUE of land within the nearest COMMUNITY containing similar ACTIVITIES, with an additional one-off road access charge of 0.001% of the value of the URBAN DEVELOPEMENT annually, times the distance in miles to the nearest COMMUNITY.

6.3.5. The SALEABLE VALUE of all land under the

responsibility of a GROUP shall be established and updated by the administrative staff of, or by an independent consultant to, the TOPMOST GROUP at least once every three years.

6.3.6. Taxes on the full cost of removing or recycling POLLUTION (such as packaging) that goes beyond the site where it was created and is not covered by insurance to render the POLLUTION harmless, shall be collected by the TOPMOST GROUP and distributed to each LEVEL GROUP under its responsibility in variable amounts in proportion to the services provided by each GROUP.

6.3.7. Any waterborne or airborne POLLUTION, radiation, electronic transmissions or excessive sound or light shall be controlled at its source in a manner that limits it from going beyond the boundary of the SITE where it is generated, unless explicitly accepted onto other SITES by those subjected to them.

6.3.8. The creator of any environmental POLLUTION from material that leaves the SITE on which it is created, shall be responsible for its safe recycling, or permanent containment when it becomes obsolete, unusable or unwanted by others outside that SITE.

6.4. Goods and Services Tax (GST)

6.4.1. Value Added GOODS AND SERVICES TAX or GST shall be set by the TOPMOST GROUP and income from the tax distributed to each LEVEL GROUP under its responsibility in variable amounts in proportion to the services provided by each GROUP.

6.4.2. Value added GST shall be payable at a single fixed percentage of the price of all sales and service transactions by the purchaser through the seller to the TOPMOST GROUP on every exchange of ownership, use or service provided.

6.4.3. The same rate of GST shall also be payable on the death of a trust director, estate owner or stock holder on the basis of the PROPORTIONAL SHARED VALUE of the assets.

6.4.4. The only exception to 6.4.2 above is that no GST shall be payable on the purchase or sale of the PRIMARY RESIDENCE of a HOUSEHOLD.

6.4.5. No INDIVIDUAL or HOUSEHOLD of that INDIVIDUAL may own more than one PRIMARY RESIDENCE at one time.

6.4.6. Personalized GST RECEIPTS shall be required for every exchange of ownership or service provided even if no money is exchanged. The receipt shall show the GST paid (if any), the date, time and location of the transaction, and the globally unique tax number of both the seller/giver and purchaser/receiver.

6.5. Dual Value of GST Receipts:

6.5.1. Every INDIVIDUAL who purchases food and/or beverages other than alcohol shall receive a separate personalized GST RECEIPT for these purchases clearly labeled with the word "FOOD" along with the IDENTIFICATION CODES of both the seller and buyer, and the other GST RECEIPT information required in Part 6.4.6. above

6.5.2. To minimize the counterfeiting of personalized GST RECEIPTS, such receipts shall be regularly randomly checked by the banking institutions accepting them and any transaction anomalies involving the seller and buyer or the date and location of the sale shall be immediately clarified by independent bank investigation.

6.5.3. Personalized GST RECEIPTS received for food and beverage purchases other than alcohol shall be considered as legal tender in the same way as other financial transactions, but may only be used to purchase the use or supply of an authorized PUBLIC UTILITY, FACILITY or SERVICE, and only after the receipt has been signed by its owner or cleared by deposit in a bank account.

6.5.4. The GST shown on personalized GST RECEIPTS received for the purchase of food and beverages (excluding alcohol) and clearly labelled "Food", may be directly used by the INDIVIDUAL purchaser who made the transaction, or by any other authorized INDIVIDUAL, to help pay any required fees for PUBLIC UTILITIES, FACILITIES AND SERVICES such as medical care and supplementary education fees.

6.5.5. Any INDIVIDUAL may authorize another INDIVIDUAL to use his or her personalized GST "Food" RECEIPT by simply signing and dating the personalized GST RECEIPT.

6.5.6. All PUBLIC UTILITIES, FACILITIES AND SERVICES must accept signed personalized GST RECEIPTS clearly labeled "Food" and any banking ENTERPRISE or INSTITUTION authorized by the TOPMOST GROUP must cash them when presented to them by a PUBLIC UTILITY, FACILITY or SERVICE.

6.5.7. Personalized GST RECEPTS shall expire on the death of the INDIVIDUAL owner of the receipts.

6.6. Social Support:

6.6.1. The following PUBLIC UTILTIES, FACILITIES AND SERVICES shall be provided through the tax revenues of the TOPMOST GROUP as redistributed to lower LEVEL GROUPS. They shall be provided to all INDIVIDUALS who use them free of charge:

6.6.1.1. The fixed land based public transportation network, excluding vehicle parking areas, but including public roads, pedestrian paths, bicycle trails, railway tracks, rail traffic management systems, train stations, marshalling yards and airports,

6.6.1.2. Public education for INDIVIDUALS to the age of 20

6.6.1.3. Health care except for initial standardized "access" charges,

6.6.1.4. Local parks,

6.6.1.5. Internal Police Forces,

6.6.1.6. Fire and Emergency Response Services,

6.6.1.7. The COURT System,

6.6.1.8. Water for drinking, cooking, cleaning and personal gardens growing food eaten by the HOUSEHOLD,

6.6.1.9. MEMBER and Administrative services for all GROUPS under the responsibility of the TOPMOST GROUP.

6.6.2. The following PUBLIC UTILTIES, FACILITIES AND SERVICES shall be funded directly by the INDIVIDUAL, paid in full or in part through the use of GST RECEIPTS:

6.6.2.1. Initial standardized access charges to public health care,

6.6.2.2. Public education from the age of 20,

6.6.2.3. Public Housing,

6.6.2.4. Major recreational facilities, such as stadiums, theatres and selected National Parks

6.6.2.5. Disability, Solo Parent, Old Age, and Retirement Benefits,

6.6.2.6. Public utilities, such as power and gas supply, sewage collection and treatment, phone services,

6.6.2.7. Metered water in excess of personal living needs,

6.6.3. For those INDIVIDUALS who are incapable of undertaking any WORK at all because of severe disabilities, those UTILTIES, FACILITIES AND SERVICES listed in 6.6.2 shall be free of charge.

6.6.4. Public health care costs shall be heavily publicly subsidized to reduce and even out delivery costs to affordable levels.

6.6.5. Public servants in positions that require a high level of cooperation among staff, such as police, school teachers and medical staff, shall not be employed using competitive methods. Employee selection shall be based on both job competency and social skills.

6.7. The Living Wage:

6.7.1. Where personal earnings are unavailable through lack of access to WORK, any ADULT or YOUNG ADULT may seek and be guaranteed WORK in the public sector at a locally set LIVING WAGE that insures basic, just and reasonable living conditions, even for the elderly and those with disabilities.

6.7.2. The LIVING WAGE shall be sufficient to allow an INDIVIDUAL'S access to public health care, safe housing, transportation, and basic recreation and entertainment facilities as well as provide for necessary food, water and energy needs.

6.7.3. The LIVING WAGE shall be distributed by the lowest possible LEVEL PUBLIC EMPLOYER, but shall be fixed at the same rate across at least the land area involved in the first three GROUP LEVELS (GL1-GL3) where the recipient lives.

6.7.4. The WORK required for an INDIVIDUAL to receive the LIVING WAGE shall be determined by the PUBLIC EMPLOYER of the lowest possible LEVEL GROUP and at his or her discretion may vary in duration or difficulty, and be fine-tuned to the particular interests, skills, age, personal commitments and abilities of each INDIVIDUAL

6.7.5. WORK at the LIVING WAGE in the public sector may involve improving public roads, parks, public utilities, schools, health care facilities, the arts or in other areas of public responsibility appropriate to an INDIVIDUAL'S health and ability, and as far as practicable in an area of the WORKER'S interest. It may also involve more personal, less traditional work such as reading to the elderly or taking care of children.

6.8. Bankruptcy:

6.8.1. When a person goes into debt for any reason and a court determines on evidence that the debt cannot be repaid as contracted, the person shall be declared a "Bankrupt".

6.8.2. The lender(s) of a Bankrupt may agree on an alternative period and means for repaying some or all of the debt on signing a new contract(s) with the debtor.

6.8.3. Unless otherwise agreed by the lender(s), repayment of a Bankrupt's debt shall require a mandatory minimum 20% deduction from all wages or other earnings of the Bankrupt for a period of 10 years or until the debt(s), including any adjustment for inflation in the locality of the debt, is paid in full.

6.8.4. Repayment of a Bankrupt's debt may include proceeds from the sale or downsizing of the person's home, car, personal possessions and/or other assets but shall not include access to social support services or the Bankrupt's LIVING WAGE.

6.8.5. Until the debt of a Bankrupt is repaid in full or to the satisfaction of all lenders, or 10 years has passed from the date of declaration, the lable of Bankrupt shall remain with the bankrupt person, and the title "Bankrupt" or "Br." shall be included before the Bankrupt's name when ever it is used in the public media or on any formal document.

6.8.6. No person declared bankrupt or within five years of its termination may have any ownership of, or management roll in, an ASSOCIATION, ENTERPRISE OR INSTITUTION.

6.9. Group Courts:

6.9.1. Every GROUP LEVEL shall establish and maintain a COURT for the purpose of hearing, judging and determining the outcome of all disputes and breaches of the RIGHTS, RESPONSIBILITIES, RULES and REGULATIONS of this CONSOCRATIC PLAN, including any civil or criminal law adopted by the GROUP as a REGULATION in this PLAN.

6.9.2. Every GROUP LEVEL (GLx) shall establish and maintain an Internal Police Force appropriate in size and duties to its responsibilities for the purpose of providing security and support according to this CONSOCRATIC PLAN for those under its responsibility.

6.9.3. Prior to the establishment of a COURT or Internal Police Force, all RIGHTS, RESPONSIBILITIES, RULES and REGULATIONS of this PLAN, including any civil, criminal or "Common" law adopted by the GROUP as a REGULATION shall be set down in writing and made public by the GROUP.

6.9.4. The ARBITER of every GROUP shall be responsible for providing liaison between his or her GROUP and the COURT.

6.9.5. The CHIEF OFFICER of every GROUP shall be responsible for providing liaison between his or her GROUP and the Internal Police Force.

6.9.6. A COURT shall be held to resolve a dispute or breach of a RIGHT, RESPONSIBILITY, RULE or REGULATION of this PLAN when an ACCUSER AFFECTED by the dispute or breach makes an application to any GROUP'S ARBITER.

6.9.7. With the CONSESUS of his or her GROUP any ARBITER may also act as an ACCUSER on any matter against any INDIVIDUAL, ASSOCIATION, ENTERPRISE, INSTITUTION or other GROUP for any reason.

6.9.8. Accusations that the ARBITER considers major or urgent, including all accusations involving death, serious mental or physical injury, rape, molestation, ABUSE or a loss valued at more than 10% of the annual LIVING WAGE, shall be referred automatically and immediately to the CHIEF OFFICER and the Internal Police Force for further investigation and any temporary remedial action needed.

6.9.9. With the CONSENSUS of the GROUP, the ARBITER may send non-urgent and minor accusations either directly to the COURT for resolution, seek additional information from the ACCUSER, refer the matter to the CHIEF OFFICER for further investigation or decline to consider the accusation.

6.9.10. If the ARBITER, with the assistance of the CHIEF OFFICER, Internal Police Force and other Administrative staff determines that the dispute or breach involves INDIVIDUALS or RESOURCES outside his or her GROUP'S area of responsibility or determines that the matter can be fully dealt with by a lower LEVEL GROUP, he or she shall immediately notify the ARBITER of the higher or lower LEVEL GROUP and forward all known information to him or her as soon as practicable.

6.9.11. Any GROUP may delegate any of its COURT or Police responsibilities under this Part to the GROUP containing its REPRESENTATIVE on the next LEVEL at any time for any reason. Any GROUP may also delegate such responsibilities to any other GROUP willing to accept them.

6.9.12. Any form of evidence, whether factual, expert or hearsay may be presented in COURT. However hearsay evidence shall be clearly identified as such at its admission to the COURT.

6.9.13. An accusation may be widened or narrowed in scope in COURT at the sole discretion of the ARBITER.

6.10. Court Accusation Procedures

6.10.1. An accusation shall be made in writing, signed by the ACCUSER and contain:

6.10.1.1. The nature of the accusation, including the, RIGHT, RESPONSIBILITY, RULE or REGULATION alleged to have been broken, or the circumstances of the dispute,

6.10.1.2. The names and contact details of the ACCUSED, where known,

6.10.1.3. The names and contact details of the ACCUSER(S),

6.10.1.4. The date(s), timing, place and other details of the setting of the dispute or breach,

6.10.1.5. A summary of the evidence in support of the accusation,

6.10.1.6. The redress sought, including any suggested monetary compensation and/or any suggested corrective measures to be applied to the ACCUSED if found guilty of the accusation.

6.10.2. Any knowingly or maliciously false statement made by an ACCUSER in any written accusation or by any INDIVIDUAL in COURT shall result in that INDIVIDUAL who makes such knowingly false or malicious accusation or statement being given the maximum redress or penalty that the ACCUSED would have faced had he or she been convicted of the breach or penalized in the dispute.

6.10.3. Where there is EVIDENCE of existing or potential violence by the ACCUSED, the ARBITOR, on the advice of the CHIEF OFFICER, may place the ACCUSED in individual "holding facilities" while the COURT determines his or her guilt or innocence.

6.10.4. Such "holding facilities" for the ACCUSED shall be secure and separate from the general public, but shall contain at least four times the minimum PRIVATE SPACE and shall allow as far as practical, the ACCUSED to communicate with anyone of his or her choosing and to have daily access to the normal comforts of private life including visitations from relatives and friends for any length of time, unless this would not be in the public interest.

6.10.5. Where there is no evidence of violence by the ACCUSED, but there is concern that he or she may abscond, ankle bracelets or other forms of electronic tags may be used to monitor and restrict movement of the ACCUSED. Incarceration is a last choice option.

6.10.6. Where there is more than one ACCUSED or one ACCUSER, all parties shall be present in COURT at the same time unless the ARBITER determines for any reason this would not achieve the most just outcome for all involved.

6.11. Rights of The Accuser and The Accused:

6.11.1. It is the choice of the ACCUSER whether an accusation is resolved through:

6.11.1.1. Direct negotiation with the ACCUSED with the assistance of an independent mutually agreed MEDIATOR, or

6.11.1.2. Trial in front of a single judge, or

6.11.1.3. Trial in front of a tribunal of three judges, or

6.11.1.3. Use of a panel looking after the interests of both the ACCUSER and the ACCUSED with the assistance of an independent mutually agreed MEDIATOR which shall include:

6.11.1.4.1. An equal number of INDIVIDUALS on the panel

known/selected by the ACCUSER and the ACCUSED, with the maximum set by the MEDIATOR of up to 6 each, and

6.11.1.4.2. Both the ACCUSER and ACCUSED present or nearby during negotiations to be able to explain their actions and to answer questions from the MEDIATOR or panel.

6.11.2. Where the decision of a COURT against an ACCUSED may involve a financial penalty greater than two year's LIVING WAGE, or restrict the movement of an ACCUSED longer than two years, The ACCUSED may request a trial by a jury of 12 randomly chosen ADULT jurors managed by a mutually agreed MEDIATOR or Judge. There is no right of either the ACCUSED or the ACCUSOR to dismiss any randomly chosen juror, Although the MEDIATOR or judge has this right.

6.11.3. The resolution of a dispute or breach through mediation shall occur only under the guidance of a trained independent MEDIATOR agreeable to both the ACCUSER and the ACCUSED

6.11.4. Both the ACCUSED and ACCUSER may choose to use Lawers and Experts for advice when involved in COURT proceedings.

6.11.5. At COURT proceedings run by a MEDIATOR, no Lawyer or Expert may speak unless directly asked by the MEDIATOR. At all other times, Lawyers and Experts may be available to the ACCUSED or ACCUSER only as a resource to be used outside the COURT room.

6.11.6. For all COURT proceedings under the jurisprudence of a judge rather than a MEDIATOR, Lawyers and Experts may be present in COURT. However the total number of Lawyers and Experts in COURT on behalf of the ACCUSED may not exceed the total number of Lawyers and experts in COURT on behalf of the ACCUSER unless the judge considers this gives an unreasonable advantage to the ACCUSER or to the ACCUSED.

6.11.7. It is the ACCUSER'S right to choose how personal evidence is presented in COURT when the ACCUSED is present, including whether it is face to face, around a blind, through a one way barrier, through electronic media (with or without distorting effects) or indirectly through the MEDIATOR, however the MEDIATOR or primary judge must concur with the ACCUSER'S choice.

6.11.8. There is no right of the ACCUSED to remain silent in COURT on the grounds that it might be self-incriminating, although every ACCUSED has the right to seek free, unbiased, publicly provided, legal advice prior to responding to police or COURT questions.

6.12. Court Decisions

6.12.1. It is the COURT'S responsibility to determine the guilt or innocence of the ACCUSED as well as the truthfulness of the ACCUSER.

6.12.2. It is the COURT'S responsibility to determine a just outcome for both the ACCUSED and ACCUSER.

6.12.3. Redress for a COURT determined OFFENCE, including for a breach of the RIGHTS, RE-SPONSIBILITIES, RULES or REGULATIONS may include any or all of the following:

6.12.3.1. Monetary reimbursement of the victim (or others) by the OFFENDER,

6.12.3.2. Confiscation of any or all existing assets of the OFFENDER,

6.12.3.3. A levee on any future income or assets of the OFFENDER, either during or after doing community service,

6.12.3.4. Mandatory and successfully completed counselling, job training, community service, and/or education achievement before release of the OFFENDER,

6.12.3.5. Banding for electronic tracking and/or incarceration (for any length of time) of the OFFENDER,

6.12.3.6. Prohibition of the OFFENDER, from undertaking any ACTIVITY, entering any SPACE, associating with any INDIVIDUAL, HOUSEHOLD, SITE, ASSOCIATION, ENTERPRISE or INSTITUTION for any period of time,

6.12.3.7. Any other punishment of the OFFENDER considered appropriate by the ARBITER with the CONSENSUS of the ARBITER'S GROUP.

6.12.4. Beyond fair compensation to the victim(s) for any loss incurred (including temporary or permanent physical or mental damage, but not including punitive damage), behavioral change shall be the sole focus of an OFENDER'S punishment.

6.12.5. Incarceration is the last choice of OFFENDER punishment, with preference first given to fair compensation for the loss to the satisfaction of all victims and restricting the movement of the OFFENDER to specific parts of a community through electronic tags or other means until all other conditions including compensation and rehabilitation are met.

6.12.6. If rehabilitation of criminal behavior cannot be achieved, incarceration or electronic tags may be permanent.

6.12.7. Until a convicted OFFENDER has met all conditions of his punishment and rehabilitation, including full repayment of the cost of any offence, an OFFENDER remains a criminal, and the title "Criminal" or "Cr." shall be included before the offender's name whenever it used in the public media, on personal contracts or on public records.

6.12.8. Where a negotiated punishment and rehabilitation agreement between the ACCUSER and ACCUSED cannot be reached, or where the agreement is not considered satisfactory by the independent MEDIATOR, the MEDIATOR shall set the final conditions of punishment and/or rehabilitation, if any, which then shall be endorsed by the ARBITOR after consultation with his or her GROUP.

6.12.9. All decisions other than successfully negotiated mediated decisions shall state the justification for that decision based on current written law.

6.12.10. COURT decisions may interpret written laws where their meaning is imprecise, but they may not create an entirely new law that is inconsistent with any current law.

6.12.11. Similar breaches may be similarly punished and/or compensated, however every case shall be considered on its own merits and there shall be no legal precedence set by any COURT decision.

6.12.12. No INDIVIDUAL may be subjected to torture or capital punishment although mechanical restraint of the OFFENDER may be appropriate for certain offences

6.12.13. The decision of a COURT against an INDIVIDUAL that involves any financial penalty greater than twice the annual LIVING WAGE or restrictions on movement longer than two years shall require the CONSENSUS of the ARBITER'S full GROUP.

6.12.14. No OFFENDER shall benefit either directly or indirectly from his or her breach of the RIGHTS, RESPONSIBILITIES, RULES or REGULATIONS of this PLAN.

6.12.15. Every action of a CHILD is the responsibility of the parent, and the parent is not only liable to compensate a victim for any expense caused by a CHILD, but may also be punished for any actions of that CHILD.

6.12.16. No INDIVIDUAL may be tried twice for the same offence unless new evidence sufficient to cast reasonable doubt on the original decision comes to hand after the original decision has been made.

6.13. Court Record keeping

6.13.1. Every accusation and all subsequent proceedings shall be recorded by the COURT and kept on record (under the appropriate IDENTIFICATION CODES) for the lifetime of both the ACCUSED and the ACCUSER.

6.13.2. All information gathered by any party during the COURT shall be available to both the ACCUSED and ACCUSER, as well as the MEDIATOR and ARBITER, and may be put in the public domain following the outcome of the COURT, unless the ARBITOR considers this inappropriate for any reason.

6.14. Pollution Management:

6.14.1. Any waterborne or airborne POLLUTION (which includes virtually all man made products), radiation, electronic transmission, sound or light must be controlled at its source in a manner that limits it from going beyond the boundary of the SITE where it is generated, unless explicitly accepted onto other SITES by those GROUPS whose AFFECTED PARTIES they represent.

6.14.2. Every end-user product that leaves the SITE on which it is created must display a permanent label on an exterior surface identifying the producers name and contact details and the total weight of each material used in the product, including packaging.

6.14.3. Every end-user product that on its own or in large quantities is harmful to the ENVIRONMENT, must be fully recycled or otherwise rendered harmless to the ENVIRONMENT by the original producer, or must be insured by a registered insurer paid for by the producer, to do the same at the end of the product's useful life.

6.14.4. Every insured end-user product must contain on the same permanent product label, the fee that will be paid by the product insurer to anyone who returns the product to any approved public waste collection point when it is no longer needed.

6.14.5. The fee paid when returning an insured waste product shall not be less than 2% of the original sales price of that product.

6.14.6. Products containing harmful materials shall substitute such materials with safer materials, however, where this is not possible all harmful materials shall be:

6.14.6.1. Fully reused, or when this is not possible:

6.14.6.2. Recovered, recycled, and/or biodegraded or when this is not possible as a last resort:

6.14.6.3. Isolated by type of contaminant and each contained in an appropriate permanent containment facility.

Part 7.   Termination:

7.1. This PLAN or any part of it may be terminated by any GROUP with the CONSENSUS of its MEMBERS.

Part 8. Interpretation:

(NOTE: All words that are written entirely in capital letters are specifically defined words, which have meanings that may be different from their customary meaning.)

ABUSE: means any violent or malicious physical or mental aggression against another INDIVIDUAL, GROUP, ASSOCIATION, ENTERPRISE or INSTITUTION and includes deliberately not upholding any GOAL, RIGHT, RESPONSIBILITY or RULE of this PLAN.

ACCESS: means the ability to move freely between a SITE and a PUBLIC PATH, and also means the landform and structures on either side of the SITE-PATH boundary that enables any INDIVIDUAL and available public utility to move freely across that boundary.

ACCUSED: means one or more INDIVIDUALS, HOUSEHOLDS, ASSOCIATIONS, ENTERPRISES, INSTITUTIONS and/or GROUPS who have been formally identify by an ACCUSER as having breached a RIGHT, RESPONSIBILITY, RULE or REGULATION of this PLAN, or who have been formally identified by an ACCUSER as being in dispute with that party.

ACCUSER: means one or more INDIVIDUALS, HOUSEHOLDS, ASSOCIATIONS, ENTERPRISES, INSTITUTIONS and/or the ARBITER of any GROUP who formally identify an ACCUSED as having breached a RIGHT, RESPONSIBILITY, RULE or REGULATION of this PLAN, or who have formally identified an ACCUSED as being in dispute with an INDIVIDUAL, HOUSEHOLD, ASSOCIATION, ENTERPRISE, or INSTITUTION.

ACTIVITY: means any use of, transmission from, consumption of or impact upon all or part of a SPACE or the environment in which it occurs by one or more INDIVIDUALS, HOUSEHOLDS, ASSOCIATIONS,

ENTERPRISES or INSTITUTIONS and includes any land, BUILDING, STRUCTURE, VEHICLE, water body or atmosphere involved in, over, under or on which the ACTIVITY occurs.

ADULT: means either 21 years old or the age at which a person meets the minimum criteria set by a GROUP for becoming an ADULT. The minimum criteria might be the person being at least 18 and holding a High School Diploma, School Certificate or other recognized life skill or accomplishment of public value.

AFFECT; means causing an EFFECT on the ENVIRONMENT.

AFFECTED PARTY: means any INDIVIDUAL, HOUSEHOLD, ASSOCIATION, ENTERPRISE or INSTITUTION that occupies a SITE where the ENVIRONMENT of that SITE is EFFECTED as a direct consequence of an ACTIVITY on another SITE.

AFFILIATION: means one or more INDIVIDUALS, HOUSEHOLDS, ASSOCIATIONS, ENTERPRISES or INSTITUTIONS who represent or express a particular interest in some aspect of personal, commercial or public interest or cause such as the right to an abortion, the right to carry a gun, the right to advertise and sell alcohol and tobacco, etc.

ALTERNATE REPRESENTATIVE: means any MEMBER who has been authorized by a GROUP to represent its interests in the absence of the GROUP'S REPRESENTATIVE. This position may be held by any GROUP MEMBER given responsibility for ENVIRONMENTAL SYSTEMS, but may not be the same sex as the REPRESENTATIVE of that GROUP.

ARBITER: means the MEMBER of a GROUP who has been selected by the GROUP to liaise with the COURT and CHIEF OFFICER and manage the judicial proceedings involving any INDIVIDUAL, HOUSEHOLD,

ASSOCIATION, ENTERPRISE or INSTITUTION under his or her responsibility in accordance with this PLAN. This position may be held by any GROUP MEMBER given responsibility for EQUITY SYSTEMS.

ASSOCIATION: means any informal collection of INDIVIDUALS who have an interest in a particular SITE or collection of SITES, whether or not such INDIVIDUALS have a financial interest in the SITE(S) or are involved in decision-making on that SITE. It includes anyone present in a single HOUSEHOLD, and any informal religious, cultural, recreational, sport, health, educational, administrative, civic or political ACTIVITY.

BUILDING: means any STRUCTURE designed for permanent or temporary occupancy by any INDIVIDUAL, animal, plant, equipment, VEHICLE or material, but does not include:

- The VEHICLE itself unless that VEHICLE is primarily used for something other than the transport of people and/or goods, such as for a DWELLING, or a place of business,
- Any temporary STRUCTURE erected for less than one month,
- Any independent deck, terrace, platform or PUBLIC PATH less than 3 feet (0.9 m) above ground level.

CHAIRPERSON: means that MEMBER of a GROUP who has been selected by the GROUP to temporarily or permanently call, organize and coordinate decision-making at GROUP meetings. This position may be held by any GROUP MEMBER given responsibility for PERSONAL SYSTEMS

CHANGE: means any new or modified ACTIVITY. It may be the result of a natural phenomenon, a human decision (or indecision whether made consciously or not), or both.

CHAOS: means the state in which movement or change appears random. Over time, however, movement or change almost always takes on a clear and identifiable form that is determined by how it begins.

CHIEF OFFICER: means that MEMBER of a GROUP who has been selected by the GROUP to liaise with the Internal Police Force, and work with the ARBITER to achieve justice and security for all INDIVIDUALS under the responsibility of the GROUP. This position may be held by any GROUP MEMBER given responsibility for EQUITY SYSTEMS

CHILD/CHILDREN: Means any person with limited social competence, due to age, mental capacity or limited exposure to education. The age that a CHILD may become a YOUNG ADULT or an ADULT is variable and dependent on the views of individual GROUPS, but is normally under 16.

COMMUNITY: means any URBAN DEVELOPMENT and the INDIVIDUALS that occupy it, which contains 10 or more HOUSEHOLDS within a single radius of 1000 feet (300 metres), and which includes any three or more of the following PUBLIC UTILITIES, FACILITIES or SERVICES: post office, school, medical facility, public administration building, public park, public water supply, public sewage collection system, community hall, sports facility, shop (any number counts as 1) , industrial activity, building used for worship, a bus or a train station. A COMMUNITY also includes any additional contiguous URBAN DEVELOPMENT outside the 1000 foot (300 meter) radius that defines the COMMUNITY.

COMMUNITY SYSTEMS means those SYSTEMS of CHANGE that involve collective human responses to the ENVIRONMENT. In general, they are larger public versions of PERSONAL SYSTEMS but by definition do not include either ECONOMIC or EQUITY SYSTEMS. COMMUNITY SYSTEMS include public media SYSTEMS, public health SYSTEMS, public education SYSTEMS, religious SYSTEMS, cultural heritage SYSTEMS, public recreation SYSTEMS and social support SYSTEMS like disability and unemployment benefits, public health insurance, public housing and retirement schemes.

CONDITIONS (of consent): means the requirements set by a GROUP that must be met by those responsible for creating or causing a CHANGE. Without limiting the scope or subject area of such requirements, they may include the documentation, preparation, source, accessibility, impact, position, access, movement, vehicle, dwelling, building, structure, size, height, volume, color, vegetation, media, cost, timing, education, health and support, as well as the cultural, social, environmental, religious, economic or public benefit of the CHANGE.

CONFLICT OF INTEREST: means, in relation to a MEMBER involved in GROUP decision-making, having knowledge of or involvement with an ACTIVITY, INDIVIDUAL, HOUSEHOLD, AFFILIATION, ASSOCIATION, ENTERPRISE or INSTITUTION, which could be seen by other MEMBERS as potentially biasing that MEMBERS views on any matter before that GROUP. This includes having any social, financial or professional involvement with any party associated with a matter before that GROUP.

CONSENSUS: means an agreement reached by a GROUP to CHANGE the status quo which no MEMBER in the GROUP opposes. An abstention is not a vote in opposition.

CONSOCRACY: means a form of representative self-government where decisions are made by STRUCTURED CONSENSUS rather than majority vote and otherwise complies with the CONSOCRATIC PLAN set out in Chapter 20 of this book.

CONSOCRATIC PLAN or PLAN: means Chapter 20 of this book.

COOPERATIVE: means any legal entity that allows INDIVIDUALS who work together to jointly and equitably share in the profits of their collaboration. INDIVIDUALS and others who live together on a single SITE and who own and run their own business solely from that SITE, operate a COOPERATIVE by definition, regardless of the actual formal structure of that business (E.g. farmers, home occupations, shopkeepers who live over their shops, etc).

CORPORATION: means any legal entity established by agreement between any number of INDIVIDUALS and a GROUP that allows the INDIVIDUAL(S) to establish, own and operate a business in the MARKET PLACE. Any number of additional INDIVIDUALS may work in the business, but all profits of the business belong solely to the INDIVIDUALS that own it.

COURT: means the formal process used to achieve Justice and resolve a dispute or breach of the RIGHTS, RESPONSIBILITIES, RULES and REGULATIONS of this PLAN under a CONSOCRACY. It includes the implementation of the justice determined by any decision reached by the COURT.

CULTURE: means the shared identity of a collection of people developed through time and association, which helps bind them together and give them a sense of collective understanding. It may include a physical place and material possessions, but these things may just remain in the shared memory of the collection of people through common symbols, rituals, language and beliefs.

DELPHI TECHNIQUE: means a decision-making methodology developed by the Rand Corporation designed to achieve a degree of CONSENSUS in a large group of people by repeatedly sharing information from each person to find common ground among all involved.

DETRIMENTAL EFFECT: means any EFFECT that causes or creates POLLUTION, involves HAZARDOUS SUBSTANCES, utilizes a NON-RENEWABLE RESOURCE, or reduces the ability for an existing ACTIVTY to continue in the same manner.

DISCRIMINATION: means any ACTIVITY of an INDIVIDUAL, GROUP, ASSOCIATION, ENTERPRISE or

INSTITUTION that prejudicially AFFECTS the lives of other INDIVIDUALS, GROUPS, ASSOCIATION, ENTERPRISE OR INSTITUTION AFFECTING their ability to live, work, communicate and/or exist with others.

ECONOMIC SYSTEMS: means those SYSTEMS that involve the private transfer of RESOURCES between SYSTEMS. The private transfer of RESOURCES can occur through RESOURCE use, work or other forms of exchange and is identified by a CHANGE in ownership or value. Such activities as banking, administration, professional services, personal services, trade, industry, construction, mining and commercial agriculture are all ECONOMIC SYSTEMS.

ECONOMIST: means that MEMBER of a GROUP who has been selected by the GROUP to monitor and assess the existing and potential effects of its decisions on the MARKET PLACE. This position is normally held by one of the MEMBERS responsible for ECONOMIC SYSTEMS, and may be held be several GROUP MEMBERS.

EFFECT: means any measurable or observable consequence of CHANGE and includes:
- any positive or adverse effect,
- any temporary or permanent effect,
- any past, present or future effect,
- any cumulative effect which arises over time or in combination with other effects regardless of the scale, intensity, duration, or frequency of the effect,
- any potential effect of high probability,
- any potential effect of low probability which has a high potential impac.

ENTERPRISE: means any ACTIVITY undertaken by any number of INDIVIDUALS, CORPORATIONS, COOPERATIVES or other businesses for profit. It includes any ACTIVITY that encourages PUBLIC ACCESS to a SITE for a profit or business related purpose.

ENVIRONMENT: means all natural and physical RESOURCES including people, land, buildings, roads, utilities, water, atmosphere, minerals, soils, light, sound, geology, flora and fauna, together with all SPACE, qualities, aesthetics, cultural values, amenity values, economic values, knowledge, beliefs (whether rational or irrational), skills, power and/or energy associated with that RESOURCE.

ENVIRONMENTALIST: means that member of a GROUP who has been selected by the GROUP to be responsible for PLANNING. This position may be held by any GROUP MEMBER given responsibility for ENVIRONMENTAL SYSTEMS.

ENVIRONMENTAL SYSTEMS: means those SYSTEMS that provide the physical setting that allows each of us to exist. They are essentially the various "eco" systems found on our globe, whether or not they contain humans or have been modified by them. They include all SYSTEMS involving natural RESOURCES such as land, water, minerals, air, plants and animals (including humans), plus all movement SYSTEMS and SYSTEMS involving physical or technological improvements added by humans such as buildings and roads (i.e. the physical attributes of civilization).

EQUITY SYSTEMS mean those SYSTEMS designed to ensure fairness, impartiality and justice. The term is not a technical reference to the residual value of encumbered property, the term's other meaning. They are SYSTEMS whose primary purpose is to maintain independent public control over the relationships that other SYSTEMS have with each other. They include our political SYSTEMS, tax systems, PLANNING & evaluation SYSTEMS, weights and measures systems, defense SYSTEMS, police SYSTEMS, legal SYSTEMS, punishment SYSTEMS and public records SYSTEMS.

FOOD: means any edible or drinkable commodity used by INDIVIDUALS to sustain life other than one containing alcohol or other mind altering drug.

FRACTAL: means having a physical shape that looks virtually the same at many different scales (sizes or magnifications).

FUNDAMENTAL RIGHTS AND RESPONSIBILITIES are those RIGHTS AND RESPONSIBILITIES that must apply to every INDIVIDUAL to allow a fully operating Consocracy to work and can only be changed by the consensus of the topmost GLT LEVEL of decision-making. They also include some RIGHTS AND RESPONSIBILITIES that are not essential to the operation of a CONSOCRACY, but are already adopted by most countries of the world as part of either the United Nations Universal Declaration of Human Rights or the Universal Islamic Declaration of Human Rights.

GOAL: means either the Goals of Humanity set out in Part 2, or any objective of PLANNING.

GROUP: means any gathering of between 6 and 42 MEMBERS who make decisions together by CONSENSUS after formally considering the five basic SYSTEMS, and who are LINKED to other GROUPS on other LEVELS.

GROUP LEVEL / GLx: means the LEVEL on which a GROUP in a STRUCTURED CONSENSUS based decision-making hierarchy makes its decisions. The (x) refers to the specified LEVEL The common names for these levels starting from LEVEL 1 is; Neighbourhood (1), Village (2), Town (3), City (4), Region (5), State (6), Country (7). Continent (8), World (9)

GST or Value Added GOODS AND SERVICES TAX: means a tax on the purchase of any tradable commodity, service or intellectual property including any RESOURCE. It is paid by the buyer based on a fixed percentage of the purchase price. However, the seller is only required to pay the collector of the tax (usually the TOPMOST GROUP) the amount received from the buyer minus the amount of tax paid by the seller to purchase or provide the original raw or wholesale goods or services.

GST RECEIPT: means the personalized receipt given by the seller of any item to the purchaser. The receipt must prominently display the amount of GST paid on the transaction and whether it was for "'FOOD", the total value of the transaction, the date, time and place of the transaction and the globally unique IDENTIFICATION CODES of both the seller and the purchaser.

HAZARDOUS SUBSTANCE: means any explosive, radioactive or bio-contaminant substance, as well as any other substance stored, used or transported in quantities of more than 100 liters or 100 kilograms with one or more of the following properties: flammability; an oxidizing nature; acute or immediate toxicity; delayed or chronic toxicity; corrosiveness or ENVIRONMENTAL persistence.

HEAD of STATE: means the REPRESENTATIVE selected by MEMBERS of the TOPMOST GROUP to represent their interest in most public situations. This position is symbolic only. The HEAD of STATE cannot make unilateral decisions.

HOUSEHOLD: means one or more INDIVIDUALS and the SITE, BUILDING and/or living SPACE he, she or they exclusively occupy. It includes all associated indoor and outdoor eating, sleeping and living SPACES of the INDIVIDUAL(S), and may include cooking, washing, toilet and storage SPACE if they are exclusive to the same INDIVIDUAL(S).

IDENTIFICATION CODE: means the globally unique number that identifies the name and associated SITE of an INDIVIDUAL. It may also identify a globally unique HOUSEHOLD, ASSOCIATION or ENTERPRISE

INDIVIDUAL: means any single human being of any age, race, religion, sex, sexual orientation, health, education and temperament. The term INDIVIDUAL includes the thoughts, actions and words of that INDIVIDUAL.

INFORMED WRITTEN CONSENT: means the consent of any AFFECTED PARTY obtained in writing after the AFFECTED PARTY has viewed all documents (or has heard described all relevant details) submitted as EVIDENCE, and has then initialed every separate document relevant to that consent.

INSTITUTION: means any non-profit organization formed to deal with an identified public need (whether real or imagined) such as any public health, education, social support, familial, communication, transportation, political, judicial, defense, religious, cultural, or resource management organization or system, and includes the ENVIRONMENT in which any such INSTITUTION operates.

INSTITUTIONAL PATERNALISM: means the belief that the INSTITUTIONS of any majority group of people are able to understand and if necessary provide for the needs of any minority group of people. (See also PATERNALISM).

INTELLECTUAL PROPERTY: means any recorded, produced, published or broadcast idea, writing, image(s), sound or transmission that is unique to any other, which has been formally identified by its creator as unique and of value. The elements of its uniqueness must be clearly identifiable by an independent qualified third party.

LAND BANKING: means obtaining rural land immediately adjacent to a COMMUNITY by that COMMUNITY well before there is any demand for it so that it can be PLANNED in advance and so that any increase in value of that land when developed may benefit the COMMUNITY as a whole rather than private enterprise.

LEADERSHIP ROLE: means any one of the 11 MEMBER roles that every GROUP is required to fill, which includes: CHAIRPERSON, PUBLICIST, ENVIRONMENTALIST, ECONOMIST, PUBLIC EMPLOYER, LOBBYIST, OMBUDSIST, ARBITER, CHIEF OFFICER, REPRESENTATIVE AND ALTERNATE REPRESENTATIVE

LEVEL: means any decision-making layer in a pyramid type organizational hierarchy. The highest numbered LEVEL (GL10+) represents the most INDIVIDUALS/SITES and the lowest numbered LEVEL (GL1) represents the fewest number of INDIVIDUALS/SITES. An INDIVIDUAL, SITE and HOUSEHOLD are below the first GL1 LEVEL,

LINK: means the sharing of information and decision-making between two GROUPS through a single INDIVIDUAL who is both a REPRESENTATIVE of one GROUP and a MEMBER of another GROUP representing the first GROUP's interests.

LIVING WAGE: means the income required by an INDIVIDUAL in exchange for WORK to allow him or her to access health care, safe housing, transportation and basic recreation and entertainment facilities as well as provide for all dependent children and necessary food, water and energy needs. The WORK required to earn a LIVING WAGE may vary in duration or difficulty, and be fine-tuned to the particular interests, skills, age, personal commitments and abilities of each INDIVIDUAL.

LOBBYIST: means the MEMBER of a GROUP that has been selected by the CONSENSUS of that GROUP to present the interests of INDIVIDUALS, HOUSEHOLDS, AFFILIATIONS, ENTERPRISES and INSTITUTIONS directly to the GROUP. This position may be held by any GROUP MEMBER given responsibility for ECONOMIC SYSTEMS.

LOOMIO: means one of several computerized methods of reaching CONSENSUS among a group of people.

MARKET PLACE: means the existing global economic system known as capitalism in which INDIVIDUALS, CORPORATIONS, COOPERATIVES, and other forms of ENTERPRISE create and provide goods and services for sale to others for profit.

MEDIATOR: means any independent neutral third party who helps all those involved in a dispute to negotiate a mutually agreeable resolution to it. The MEDIATOR should preferably be a judge with personal experience and training in mediation techniques, although this is not mandatory if the MEDIATOR is known and trusted by both the ACCUSED and ACCUSER.

MEMBER: means a REPRESENTATIVE who has joined another GROUP and has attended that GROUP'S meetings and responded to other MEMBER questions for at least six meetings of that GROUP. In a CONSOCRACY all MEMBERS provide a LINK to lower LEVEL GROUPS while the REPRESENTATIVE of that GROUP provides a LINK to one other GROUP usually on the next higher LEVEL.

NODES / NODAL GROWTH: means a form of URBAN DEVELOPMENT where PUBLIC FACILITIES AND SERVICES are clustered together around PUBLIC transportation terminals (usually rail) and the density of development increases toward the center of that cluster. The most intensively developed areas include multi-use PUBLIC gathering places linked together by pedestrian paths. VEHICLE movement, ACCESS and parking should all be isolated from such PATHS.

OFFENDER: means any INDIVIDUAL, ASSOCIATION, ENTERPRISE, INSTITUTION or GROUP who or which has been found in a GROUP COURT to have breached a RIGHT, RESPONSIBILITY, RULE or REGULATION of the CONSOCRACY or to have been ABUSIVE against another INDIVIDUAL. ASSOCIATION, ENTERPRISE, INSTITUTION or GROUP.

OFFENSIVE or OBJECTIONABLE: means any deliberately provocative, insensitive or inflammatory language, images, structures, sounds or smells.

OMBUDSIST: (customarily called Ombudsman) means that member of a GROUP who has been selected by the CONSENSUS of the GROUP to provide an independent PUBLIC assessment of lower LEVEL GROUP decisions for those eligible MEMBERS who request it. This position may be held by any GROUP MEMBER given responsibility for PERSONAL SYSTEMS.

PATERNALISM: means a relationship between two or more INDIVIDUALS or GROUPS where one is considered more important than the other(s), such as a parent to a child or a teacher to a student. The inequality may be due to a difference in age, knowledge, skills or experience, but it can also be due to a difference in power, money or respect. See also INSTUTIONALISED PATERNALISM.

PERMITTED ACTIVITY: means any ACTIVITY which fully complies with the Performance Standards set out in these Rules, or any ACTIVITY which has been specifically approved by the GROUP responsible for controlling the EFFECTS of that ACTIVITY.

PERSONAL SYSTEMS: means those SYSTEMS that are unique to an individual and arise from the actions of a person's own body, mind, character, experience and response to the environment around him or her. Such SYSTEMS include those involving the consumption of food, the occupation of shelter, the establishment and maintenance of friendships, the procreation and nurturing of children, the ownership of physical and intellectual property, the pursuit of pleasure and happiness, the feeling and expression of emotions, and the perception of the five bodily senses. By definition, however, they exclude ECONOMIC and EQUITY SYSTEMS.

PLANNING: Means the intellectual process of determining when, why and how to influence CHANGE for the public good. It contains the following steps:

1. Identify what the future state should be; that is, set the GOALS,

2. Identify and clarify of the problems that may interfere with achieving these GOALS, and the opportunities that may achieve them quicker or with fewer resources,

3. Identify and analyse (including side effects) alternative ways to solve the problems and utilize the opportunities to achieve the GOALS,

4. Select the best way to do this; that is, come up with a "Plan",

5. Implement "The Plan",

6. The monitoring of subsequent change and if the results are not as expected, revise "The Plan" (or alternatively, modify the GOALS).

PLEASURE DRUGS: means any mind altering drug or activity that enables INDIVIDUALS to escape from reality and includes alcohol, opiates such as morphine, heroin, and codeine, cocaine and its derivative crack, LSD, barbiturates, cannabis, caffeine, nicotine, kava, chat and beetle nut. It also may include gambling, computer gaming and other addictions when they interfere with normal human responses to the ENVIRONMENT.

POLLUTION: means any consequence or product of an ACTIVITY whether alone or cumulatively that reduces the ability of the ENVIRONMENT to sustain life indefinitely. This includes all goods and structures unless they rapidly biodegrade and leave the ENVIRONMENT unchanged.

POSSIBLE RIGHTS AND RESPONSIBILITIES: means those RIGHTS AND RESPONSIBILITIES that any GROUP of people may modify or remove at any time to suit themselves by the CONSENSUS of those in their GROUP. They are included as possible RIGHTS AND RESPONSIBILITIES because they might be helpful to manage specific GROUPS or help achieve CONSENSUS among divergent opinions. Because of religious, cultural, political or other conflicts, they may not be appropriate to use in every GROUP.

PRIMARY RESIDENCE: means the HOUEHOLD where an INDIVIDUAL sleeps most often in any 12 month period. It includes the SITE on which that HOUSEHOLD is located.

PRIVATE LAND: means any SITE which is legally owned by one or more INDIVIDUALS for their own exclusive use and enjoyment. It may include rental property for exclusive use by those the SITE owners choose but it does not include any SITE which contains an ENTERPRISE that directly involves the PUBLIC.

PRIVATE PROPERTY: means any physical or intellectual item that is legally accessible to only one person or to a clearly defined group of people such as a family or a corporation. Limited accessibility may be the result of accepted usage, force or legal title.

PRIVATE SPACE: means an exclusive three-dimensional sheltered SPACE with access to sunlight and natural air, of sufficient size to allow an INDIVIDUAL to stand and lie down in private with limbs fully extended in all directions (approximately 500 ft3 or 15 m3 of three-dimensional space with a minimum dimension of 8 feet or 2.4 metres).

PROBATIONARY MEMBER: means a REPRESENTATIVE who has joined a new GROUP and has not yet attended at least six meetings and responded to MEMBER questions of that GROUP if asked in these meetings.

PROPORTIONAL SHARED VALUE: means the value of an INDIVIDUAL'S estate including material goods and possessions, cash, stocks, bonds, and intellectual property rights as if that estate were distributed among all owners, directors, stockholders and Trustees of that estate immediately prior to the INDIVIDUAL'S death in proportion to its financial value to each party.

PUBLIC: means accessible to and/or involving all INDIVIDUALS all the time, without exception.

PUBLICIST: means that MEMBER of a GROUP who has been selected by the GROUP to be responsible for publicly notifying and recording all meetings and all decisions reached, as well as formally providing the MEDIA with all information regarding the ACTIVITIES of the GROUP. This position may be held by any GROUP MEMBER given responsibility for COMMUNITY SYSTEMS.

PUBLIC LAND: means any SITE that is occupied by a publicly owned INSTITUTION.

PUBLIC MEDIA: means any object, sound or transmission device or service including a human voice, which is used to advertise, display, identify or inform (including radio, television, telephones, SIGNS, newspapers, magazines or the internet), and which is distributed to, or which can be seen, heard or understood by an INDIVIDUAL outside the SITE on which it is generated.

PUBLIC PATH or PATH: means all PUBLIC LAND primarily used for the movement of people and goods between SITES. It includes all footpaths, roads, railroads, navigable waterways and airports, and all STRUCTURES on a PUBLIC PATH, such as bridges, doorways, enclosures and harbors. It also includes all walkways, hallways and corridors on PRIVATE LAND used for PUBLIC access including those within any private building containing one or more SITES.

PUBLIC SPACE: means any SPACE or ACTIVITY that is equally available to all INDIVIDUALS within the same GROUP or COMMUNITY. It includes PRIVATE LAND that contains an ENTERPRISE that is PUBLIC

RECOMMENDED RIGHTS AND RESPONSIBILITIES: means those RIGHTS AND RESPONSIBILITIES that should be adopted to encourage peaceful co-existence between people, achieve social justice or promote ENVIRONMENTAL SUSTAINABILITY. They are not fundamental to the operation of a CONSOCRACY, but they could significantly improve its operation. They may be modified or removed by the CONSENSUS of any GROUP.

REGISTER OF PUBLIC SERVANTS: means a printed and electronic record available to the PUBLIC of all MEMBERS of a GROUP, all Administrative staff used by the GROUP, all staff of all PUBLIC UTILITIES, FACILITIES and SERVICES administered by the GROUP and all consultants that provide advice to either the GROUP or their staff. The register shall contain their full names and personal details including IDENTIFICATION CODE, photo ID and Curriculum Vitae.

REGULATION: means any additional RULE made to clarify or expand upon any existing RIGHT, RESPONSIBILITY or RULE in this PLAN. A REGULATION may be made by any GROUP for any reason including clarifying the timing or method of implementation or any other relevant matter, provided the original meaning of the RIGHT, RESPONSIBILITY or RULE is not altered.

REPRESENTATIVE: means any INDIVIDUAL MEMBER of a GROUP that is selected by the CONSENSUS of that GROUP to represent its interests and make decisions on its behalf in a second GROUP (usually, but not always on the next higher LEVEL). In the second GROUP that REPRESENTATIVE loses the title of REPRESENTATIVE and becomes just a MEMBER of the second GROUP. If that MEMBER then is selected by the second GROUP to represent its interest in yet another (third) GROUP, his or her association with the first GROUP automatically ends, and thus cannot be removed by that GROUP. In the TOPMOST GROUP the REPRESENTATIVE is the HEAD of STATE

RESOURCE: means any natural or man-made, temporary or permanent substance, feature, life form, situation or INTELLECTUAL PROPERTY that has economic, social, environmental, spiritual, cultural or emotional value to an INDIVIDUAL. It includes human beings themselves.

RESOURCE MANAGEMENT: means Managing the use, development and protection of natural and physical resources in a way, or at a rate which enables people and communities to provide for their social, economic, and cultural well-being and for their health and safety while-

• Sustaining the potential of natural and physical resources to meet the reasonably foreseeable needs of future generations; and

• Safeguarding the life-supporting capacity of air, water, soil, and ecosystem; and

• Avoiding, remedying or mitigating any adverse effects of activities on the ENVIRONMENT.

RIGHTS AND RESPONSIBILITIES: means the rights and responsibilities listed in Part 4 of this PLAN. See also FUNDAMENTAL RIGHTS RECOMMENDED RIGHTS, and POSSIBLE RIGHTS

RULE: means any agreed SYSTEM or pattern of human behavior adopted by a CONSOCRACY to legally achieve an agreed Goal, Right or Responsibility, and includes Parts 5, 6, 7 & 8 of this PLAN.

RURAL LAND: means any SITE or any undefined area of land or water body used for pastoral, horticulture, forestry, aqua culture, crops or similar agricultural activity (including temporarily fallow land), any land or water body in its undisturbed natural state or any land that has been regenerating to its natural state for at least the last five years. It does not include any SITE occupied by a BUILDING, HOUSEHOLD, ASSOCIATION, ENTERPRISE or INSTITUTION.

SAFE SITE: means any SITE that has been publicly identified as a "Safe Site" for use by INDIVIDUALS who seek or require special management of their behavior. It may be used by those who wish to gamble, seek a prostitute, shoot special guns or use a strong PLEASURE DRUG, among others. A SAFE SITE may only be entered voluntarily, but departure is permitted only if the INDIVIDUAL is free of the restricted material and fully able to function outside the SAFE SITE with no measureable amount of restricted drug within his or her body. A SAFE SITE may include a private home, business or even a defined public area where there are appropriate controls to ensure continued confinement of the INDIVIDUAL if necessary.

SALEABLE VALUE: means the value of land sold on the open market if all buildings or other structures (if any) on the land are removed, but the location or other characteristics of the land remain unchanged.

SITE: means any SPACE or collection of contiguous SPACES which is entirely under the control of one or more INDIVIDUALS HOUSEHOLDS, ASSOCIATIONS, ENTERPRISES or INSTITUTIONS. As a minimum, it provides exclusive private three-dimensional shelter with direct human access to a public path, sunlight and natural air for one ADULT and allows that ADULT to stand and lie down with limbs fully extended in any direction, or approximately 500 ft3 or 15 m3 of three-dimensional space with a minimum dimension of 8 feet or 2.4 meters. It includes PUBLIC LAND and PRIVATE LAND whose boundaries are recorded in public records, or whose boundaries are reasonably distinguishable by natural or physical changes in landscape, material composition, surface texture or other obvious visual feature that can be used to define ownership or occupancy. It may involve SPACE not at ground level such as a room or collection of rooms in a BUILDING and it may involve distinguishable portions of water areas, such as harbors and flood plains. Any SITE described in public records in only two dimensions, such as land ownership titles, shall be deemed to contain a third, vertical dimension which includes all existing STRUCTURES situated on that two dimensional SPACE, and in addition extends not less than ten metres below and ten metres above ground level unless a greater or lesser interpretation is clearly obvious by a STRUCTURE within that SPACE.

SOCIOCRACY; means a method for reaching CONSENSUS decisions among a diverse group of people first developed in The Netherlands in the 1920s by pacifist Keese Boek. The Term "GROUP" in this plan is very similar to how the term "circle" is used in sociocracy.

SPACE: means any two dimensional area or any three dimensional volume.

SUB-GROUP: means any ASSOCIATION, ENTERPRISE or INSTITUTION that is LINKED directly or indirectly to a GROUP,

SUB-GROUP LEVEL GLxSy: means a SUB-GROUP on a specific numbered LEVEL of a STRUCTURED CONSENSUS based decision-making hierarchy.. The (x) refers to the specific SUB-GROUP LEVEL, and the (y) refers to the SUB-GROUP name.

STRUCTURE: means any physical object found in the ENVIRONMENT, whether movable or immovable, temporary or permanent, which is composed of materials that are not in their original, naturally occurring state, and includes impounded water and excavations.

STRUCTURED CONSENSUS: means a form of CONSENSUS decision-making where large numbers of INDIVIDUALS voluntarily collect themselves into many small GROUPS of a size that allows each GROUP to reach all its decisions by the CONSENSUS of its MEMBERS, and where each of these first LEVEL GROUPS then selects by CONSENSUS one REPRESENTATIVE from among themselves to represent their interests in a second LEVEL GROUP. each new GROUP being of a size that allows its MEMBERS to reach decisions by CONSENSUS. Additional LEVELS of GROUPS are formed In a like manner as needed until the TOPMOST GROUP contains only one GROUP of between 6 an 42 MEMBERS. All decision-making is undertaken by the lowest LEVEL GROUP able to fully represent the interests of all those INDIVIDUALS and the ENVIRONMENT AFFECTED by a CHANGE.

SUSTAINABLE ENVIRONMENT or ENVIRON-MENTAL SUSTAINABILITY: means the state of RESOURCE use and management in which the life-supporting capacity of air, water, soil, and ecosystems are safeguarded for future generations, and in which the health and safety of INDIVIDUALS and their social, economic, and cultural well-being are provided for in perpetuity.

SUSTAINABLE RESOURCE: means any RESOURCE which is used in a way or at a rate that does not reduce the ability of future generations to use it in the same way.

SYSTEM (SYSTEM of CHANGE): means any ACTIVITY, INDIVIDUAL, HOUSEHOLD, AFFILIATON, ASSOCIATION, ENTERPRISE, INSTITUTION, STRUCTURE, belief or process that manipulates a physical or intellectual RESOURCE in a predictable way. Unless the process involves only natural resources, it includes some form of human decision-making. There are five basic types of SYSTEMS (of change): PERSONAL, ECONOMIC, EQUITY, COMMUNITY and ENVIRONMENTAL. .
Note: The way the term "system" is used here is similar to, but not the same as how Biologist Ludwig Von Bertalanffy used the term for his "System's Theory" back in the 1940s. He used the term to describe the multiplying effect of interlinked change on the whole, while the term as used in this plan simply describes any process that includes or results in change.

TAKING: means the forced acquisition of PRIVATE PROPERTY or private rights by a GROUP for some public purpose, such as a new public road or sewerage system.

TOPMOST GROUP: means the single GROUP of MEMBERS on the highest LEVEL of a CONSOCRACY. At least five of its MEMBERS must each advocate one of the 5 identified sets of SYSTEMS, namely Personal, Economic, Equity, Community and Environmental Systems. One of the remaining MEMBERS shall become HEAD of STATE

TYRANNY OF THE MAJORITY: means that even in the best democracies it only takes 51 percent of those involved in any decision to decide the fate of the other 49 percent. It is assumed that the institutions of any majority group can fully understand and if necessary provide for the needs of any minority group, which is simply not true. This serious shortcoming of democratic decision-making was foreseen but ulltimately left unresolved 250 years ago by Adams, Madison, Mill, Tocqueville and others whose ideas helped form the US Consititution.

URBAN DEVELOPMENT: means any collection of one or more BUILDINGS containing one or more INDIVIDUALS, HOUSEHOLDS, ASSOCIATIONS, ENTERPRISES or INSTITUTIONS, along with the associated land they occupy. It does not include any SITE or undefined area of land or water body used solely for outdoor pastoral, horticulture, forestry, aqua culture, crops or similar outdoor agricultural activity (including temporarily fallow land), any land or water body in its undisturbed natural state or any land that has been regenerating to its natural state for at least the last five years.

UTILITY, FACILITY and SERVICE: means ACTIVITIES provided by an INSTITUTION or an accredited ENTERPRISE for PUBLIC use and includes PUBLIC PATHS, electricity, gas, water and sewer supply, distribution and treatment networks, COURTS. Internal Police Forces, Fire Services, Emergency Services, parks and recreation facilities, schools and health care facilities.

VALUE KNOWLEDGE MANAGEMENT: means a computerized method developed by Dr. John Rohrbaugh of reaching CONSENSUS among a group of people with very diverse interests.

VEHICLE: means any motorised device used for transportation such as automobile, truck, bus, van, recreational vehicle, motorcycle, tractor, train, plane, helicopter, rocket, boat, hovercraft, or motorised bicycle, scooter, skateboard, other than transport devices which are physically incapable of move faster than 5 mph (8 kph).

VIOLENCE: means any vicious or abusive behaviour that involves malicious physical or mental aggression against another person or group. The drive to violence and abuse is often driven by the offender's belief that such behavior is his (or her) right when reacting against something they don't like or don't understand.

WORK: means any legal ACTIVITY which provides fair compensation for an INDIVIDUAL'S mental or physical effort. The WORK required to earn a LIVING WAGE may vary significantly in duration or difficulty according to the particular age, mental ability, physical skills, education, experience, interests, and personal commitments of each INDIVIDUAL.

YOUNG ADULT: means either 18 years old or the age at which a CHILD meets the minimum criteria set by a GROUP for becoming a YOUNG ADULT. The minimum criteria might be the person being at least 16 and having reading and writing competency in the GROUPS primary language.

Partial Bibliography

This partial bibliography contains some of the books that currently sit on the shelf above my desk. I have used them and the internet extensively to write this Plan, but many other resources found in distant libraries, among friends and on TV are now lost from memory.

- Alexander, Christopher, A Timeless Way of Building, Oxford University Press, USA, 1979.
- Alexander, Christopher, Hajo Neis, Artemis Anninou, A New Theory of Urban Design, Oxford University Press, USA, 1987.
- Alexander, Christopher, Sara Ishikawa, Murray Silverstein, Max Jacobson, Ingrid Fiksdahl-King and Shlomo Angel, A Pattern Language, Towns-Buildings-Construction, Oxford University Press, USA, 1977.
- Allott, Stephen, Friends in Oxford, The history of a Quaker Meeting, Grants Hill Press, Somerset, 1952.
- Anon (Baha'i World Center), The Promise of World Peace, National Spiritual Assembly of the Baha'i, Auckland, 1985.
- Avery, Michael, Building United Judgment: A Handbook for Consensus Decision Making, Create Space, 1999
- Berk, Emanuel, Downtown Improvement Manual, ASPO Press, Chicago, 1976.
- Breines, Simon, William j. Dean, The Pedestrian Revolution Streets Without Cars, Vintage Books Random House, New York, 1974.
- Bregman, Rutger, Utopia for Realists, and How We Get There, Bloomsbury Publishing, London, 2018
- Bryson, Bill, A Short History of Nearly Everything, Black Swan Transworld, London, 2004.
- Buck, John, Sharon Villines, We The People, Consenting to a Deeper Democracy, Sociocracy.info, Lightning Source, UK ltd, 2007
- Chermayeff, Serge, Christopher Alexander, Community and Privacy, Toward a New Architecture of Humanism, Anchor Books Doubleday and Co, New York, 1965.

- Chomsky, Noam, Hegemony or Survival, America's Quest for Global Dominance, Metropolitan Owl Book Henry Holt and Co, New York, 2004.
- Chomsky, Noam, Hopes and Prospects, Penguin Group NZ a Pearson Group, Rosedale North Shore, 2010.
- Chomsky, Noam, *Who Rules the World*, Hamish Hamilton Penguin, 2016.
- Chomsky, Noam and C.J.Polychroniou, *Optimism over Despair*, Penguin Randomhouse UK, 2017.
- Choudhury, Golam W. The Prophet Muhammad, His life and Eternal Message, Scorpion Publishing Ltd, Essex, England, 1993.
- Cookson, J. W. (Minister), Hazardous Waste Management and Disposal, Government of Alberta, Edmonton, 1979.
- Cornford, Francis MacDonald, The Republic of Plato, Oxford University Press, New York, 1966.
- Crowther, Sir Geoffrey, Traffic in Towns The Specially Shortened Edition of the Buchanan Report, Penguin Books, Baltimore, 1964.
- DeChiara, Joseph, Lee Koppelman, Urban Planning and Design Criteria, Van Nostrand Reinhold Company, New York, 1975.
- Deloria Jr, Vine, Clifford M Lytle, The Nations Within, Pantheon Books, New York, 1984.
- McNichols, W.M. Jr (Mayor), Automobile Diversion A Strategy for Reducing Excessive Traffic in Sensitive Areas, Denver Planning Office, Denver, 1978.
- Dicken, Samuel N, Forest R Pitt, Introduction to Human Geography, Blaisdell Publishing Co, New York, 1963.
- Durning, Alan Thein, How Much is Enough, Earthscan Publications, London, 1992.
- Elder, Neil, Thomas, Alastair H and Arter, David, "The Consensual Democracies? Martin Robertson and Co, Oxford, 1982.
- Engwicht, David, Towards an Eco-City, Calming the Traffic, Envirobook, Sydney, 1992.
- Epstein, David F. The Political Theory of The Federalist, University of Chicago Press, Chicago, 1984.

- Fein, Albert, Frederick Law Olmsted and the American Environmental Tradition, George Braziller Inc, New York, 1973.
- Fletcher, Banister, A History of Architecture on the Comparative Method, Charles Scribner's Sons, New York, 1963.
- Fraser, Douglas, Village Planning in the Primitive World, Studio Vista, London, c.1970.
- Fullard, H, H.C. Darby, The University Atlas 22nd Edition, George Philip & Son, Ltd, London, 1983
- Giedion, Sigfried, Space Time and Architecture The growth of a New tradition, Harvard University Press, Cambridge, 1959,
- Gist, Noel P. Sylvia Fleis Fava, Urban Society, Thomas Crowell Company, New York, 1964.
- Goodman, Robert, After the Planners, Penguin Books Compton Printing, Aylesbury, 1972.
- Graeber, David and Rutger Bregman, TheThe Dawn of Everything, A New History of Humanity", Allen Lane/ Penguin. 2021
- Harger, Nicky, Bob Burton, Secrets and lies, Craig Potton Publishing, Nelson, NZ. 1999
- Hardoy, Jorge, Urban Planning in Pre-Columbian America, Studio Vista, London, c.1970.
- Heilbroner, Robert L. The Worldly Philosophers The Lives, Times and Ideas of Great Economic Thinkers, Touchstone Simon and Schuster, New York, 1992.
- Herman, Chomsky, Manufacturing Consent, Vintage UK, Random House. London, 1994,
- Hoff, Benjamin, The Tao of Pooh, Viking Penguin, New York, 1983.
- Jacobs, Jane, The Death and Life of Great American Cities, Vintage Books Random House, New York, 1963.
- James, Preston E. A Geography of Man, Gin and Company, New York, 1959.
- Kaplan, Robert D. The Coming Anarchy, Shattering the Dreams of the Post Cold War, Random House, New York, 2000.

- Karsten, Frank, Karel Beckman, Beyond Democracy, ICG Testing.Com. 2012
- Kitchen, Paddy, A Most Unsettling Person, The life and Ideas of Patrick Geddes, Saturday review Press E.P. Dutton, USA, 1975.
- Kraus, Chris, Sylvere Kitrubger Hatred of Capitalism, Semiotext(e) MIT Press, Los Angeles, 2001.
- Kraybill, Donald B., The Riddle of the Amish Culture, The Johns Hopkins University Press, Baltimore, 1991.
- Last, Geoffrey, Richard Pankhurst, Eric Robeson, A History of Ethiopia in Pictures, Oxford University Press, Addis Ababa, 1969.
- Landers, Howard M. Miniparks, Denver Planning Office, Denver, 1968.
- Lipton, Bruce, SteveBhaerman, Spontaneoud Evolution; Our Positive Future and a way to get there from Here, Hay House, USA 2009
- Lynch, Kevin, The Image of the City, MIT Press, Cambridge, 1966.
- Mair, Lucy, Primitive Government, A Study of Traditional Political Systems in Eastern Africa, Indiana University Press, Bloomington, 1977.
- Meadows, Donella H, Dennis L Meadows, Joergen Randers, William W. Dehrens III, Limits to Growth, Signet Classics New American Library, New York, 1975.
- McLean, Mary, Local Planning Administration, The International City Managers Association, Chicago, 1959.
- Miliband, Ed, *"GO BIG, How to Fix the World"* Vintage, 2021.
- Moorehead, Alan, The Blue Nile, First Four Square Edition, London, 1969.
- Moore, Michael, Stupid White Men, Harper Collins, New York, 2001.
- Morford, Mark, The Daring Spectacle, Adventures in deviant Journalism, Rapture Machine Inc, San Francisco, 2010.
- Morrison, Roy, We Build the Road as we Travel, New Society Publishers, Philadelphia, 1991.
- Mumford, Lewis, City Development, Studies in

Disintegration and Renewal, Secker and Warburg, London, 1946.

- Mumford, Lewis, Sticks and Stones, A Study of American Architecture and Civilization, 2nd edition, Dover Publications, New York, 1955.
- Muschanp, David, Political Thinkers, St Martin's Press, New York, 1986.
- Nearing, Scott, The Conscience of a Radical, Social Science Institute, Harborside, Maine, 1967.
- Pevsner, Nikolaus, Pioneers of Modern Design from William Morris to Walter Gropius, Penguin Books, Norwich, 1966.
- Poole A.L. Land Use Capability Survey Handbook, Ministry of Works, Wellington, N.Z. 1974
- Poteete, Janssen, Ostrom, Working Together, Collective Action, the Commons and Multiple Methods in Practice, Princeton University Press, Princeton, New Jersey, 2010
- Purdy, Barry I, Shopping Areas: Planning and Capital Investment in Retailing, NZ Retailers' Federation Inc, 1981.
- Rackham, H. Aristotle, The Nicomachean Ethics, Harvard University Press, Cambridge, 2003.
- Rau, Ted J. Who Decides Who Decides: Sociocracyforall.org, 120 Pulpit Road, Amherst, MA, 01002.
- Rau, Ted J. and Jerry Koch-Gonzales, Many Voices One Song – Shared Power with Sociocracy, Sociocracyforall.org, Lightning Source UK Ltd
- Schumacher, E.F., Small is Beautiful, Economics as if People Mattered, Harper and Row, New York, 1973.
- Soleri, Paolo, Arcosanti an Urban Laboratory? VTI Press, Santa Monica, 1987.
- Thoreau, Henry David, Walden, or Life in the Woods and On the Duty of Civil Disobedience, Signet Classic Penguin Books, USA, 1960.
- Turnbull, Collin M. The Mountain People, Simon and Schuster, New York, 1972.
- Wiebenson, Dora, Tony Garnier: The Cite Industrielle, Studio Vista, London, c.1970.
- Wells, Carolyn, Mary Ann Suppes, The Social Work

Experience 7th Edition, Pearson Education Ltd. 2018
- Wells, Helen Ann McLaren, *Rough Draft, The Story of Your Mother's Life,* Self published, Apia, Samoa, 2006
- Wells, Ian Cressy, *The Orientation and Cognition of Objects,* Doctorate Thesis, Univeristy of Auckland, NZ, 2010
- Wells, Rosemary, Thomas Wells, The House in the Mail, Viking, 2002
- Wells, Tao, Easier on, Govett-Brewster Art Gallery, New Plymouth, NZ, 2018
- Wells, Ted, *Identification of Possible Future Lifestyle Areas,* New Plymouth District Council, 2010
- Wells, Ted, *Lamunin Local Area Plan,* Kerajaan Negara Brunei Darussalam, Jurutara Damit Beca Consultants, Brunei, 1996
- Wells, Ted, The Old Man in the Bag and Other True Stories of Good Intentions, CreateSpace, NC, USA, 2012
- Wells, Ted, *Porgera Master Plan,* Porgera Development Authority, Beca Gure Consultants, Porgera, Papua New Guinea, 1998
- Wells, Ted, *Power, Chaos & Consensus, Consocratic Theory,* CreateSpace, NC, USA, 2012
- Wells, Ted. *Stage II Site Study,* Ministry of Works and Development, New Plymouth, NZ, June 1984
- Wells, Ted. *Sussex County Long-Range Transportation Plan Update,* Delaware Department of Transportation, Kise, Straw and Kolodner Consultants, Dover, Delaware, 2001
- Wells, Ted, *Taranaki Rural Land Resource Priorities Study,* Ministry of Works and Development, New Plymouth, NZ, 1987.
- Wells, Ted. *Vaitele Urban Governance Pilot Project,* Ministry of Natural Resources and Environment, Samoa, 2010
- Wills, Gary, The Federalist Papers by Alexander Hamilton, John Jay and James Madison, Bantam Doubleday Dell, New York, 1982.

Partial list of Website Addresses Accessed

Allen, Christopher, http://www.lifewithalacrity.com/
Brown, Craig, https://info.commondreams.org/
Buck, John, http://www.governancealive.com/
Eckstein, Juta, https://www.agilebossanova.com/
Francois Knuchel, http://sociocracyuk.ning.com/
Hennig, Dr, Brett, https://www.sortitionfoundation.org/
John, Edwin M. www/linkedin.com/in/edwin-john-70499b31
and   http://www.childrenparliament.in/aboutus.html
Johnson, Danny, https://myodemocracy.org/
Kudumbashree, http://www.kudumbashree.org/
Rau, Ted, https://www.sociocracyforall.org/
Robertson, Brian, https://www.holacracy.org/
Villines, Sharon, John Buck https://www.sociocracy.info/
Wales, Jimmy, Sanger, Larry, https://en.wikipedia.org/wiki/

Partial List of Documentaries Viewed

Achbar, Mark, Peter Wintonick, Manufacturing Consent, Noam Chomsky and the Media, 1992

Bakan, Joel, Mark Achbar and Jennifer Abbott. Directors, The Corporation, 2003

Fothergill, Alastar, Director, Jonnie Hughes, Et al. Sir David Attenborough, A Life on our Planet, Silverback Films, 2020

Gibney, Alex. Director et al, Enron, The Smartest Guys in the Room, 2005

Jarecki, Eugene, Director, Why We fight, Sony Picture Classics, 2005

Orlowsky, Jeff, Director, The Social Dilemma, Netflix Film, 2020

Paine, Chris, Director, Who Killed the Electric Car? Sony Picture Classics, 2006

Winterbottom, Michael, Director, *The Emperor's New Clothes,* IFC Films, 2015

Synopsis by Chapter

Power, Chaos or Consensus?
How to Fix our Global Melt-Down:
A PLAN FOR THE PLANET

Part A: Introducing the Global Puzzle

Chapter 1: The Ethiopian Connection: explains when and where the ideas about fixing the planet originated. It begins by explaining two observations made during the 3 years Ted and his wife, Helen, were volunteers helping a few dozen very poor, uneducated but very intelligent Amhara farmers clear jungle and start a new town in an extremely remote part of southern Ethiopia back in the late 1960s. The land had been personally given to them by the elderly, god-like Emperor, Haile Selassie, also an Amhara.

Chapter 2: Is the Answer Really 42?: was written more than 30 years ago when Ted tried to clarify what he hoped to accomplish writing this book, which he had started two decades earlier. At the time, the New Zealand Government had almost gone bankrupt and the author was only *beginning to understand that the objectives of a successful market place, a just society and a sustainable environment* have almost nothing in common with each other.

Chapter 3: Making Public Decisions with Guns and Money: discusses two of the primary ways existing governments now make decisions; through war or its threat, and through the market place. It includes a UN chart which obliquely points out that over the last 20 years the USA could have unilaterally ended virtually all of the major problems facing humanity on this planet, by providing clean water, clean energy, food, education, health care and housing to literally every one in need on the planet, along with stopping climate change, eliminating all land mines and nuclear weapons, and paying off all developing nation debt, had it used just part of its existing military budget to help the world rather than fight it "defending democracy".

Chapter 4: Other Ways We Make Public Decisions: discusses Aristotle's six forms of government including Democracies, which the Greek philosopher describes as a "corruption". It also describes New Zealand's unique form of government which has no permanent over-riding constitution, no publicly elected head of state and only one legislative chamber, forty percent of whose members are not publicly elected.

Chapter 5: The Delphi Technique: is about how Ted helped a very diverse range of technical experts, government officials, industry representatives and more than two dozen social, cultural and environmental organizations work together to identify the site for a very contentious major petrochemical complex in New Zealand following the discovery of natural gas off-shore there.

Chapter 6: Lessons From The South Pacific: is about the centuries old Samoan practice of making community decisions by consensus. It is where the author learned first hand during several years living and working among the local people there trying to plan for climate change induced sea level rise, that it does not require unanimous or even majority support to make consensus decisions.

Chapter 7: The Key: describes how consensus decision-making could be made to work in groups involving thousands, even billions of people by using a simple "linked" multi-level structure of decision-making.

Chapter 8: In Search of the "Big Picture": tries to make sense of the incredible complexity of today's world. Eventually five significant pieces of the puzzle are uncovered involving Personal, Economic, Equity, Community and Environmental change.

Chapter 9: So Where Should We Be Headed?: looks at all the goals that various religions, cultures and governments have set out for people to live by over the last several millennia starting with Moses, Siddhartha Gautama and Confucius.

Part B: The Problems We Face

Chapter 10: The Complexity of our Current Mess: suggests that while the United Nations and other governments have brief lists of human rights for us all to live by, these lists are not nearly detailed enough to describe how humanity on this planet might get out of the deep mess it's in.

Chapter 11: Personal Problems: discusses sixteen problems involving personal matters that governments often try to control without any detailed understanding of their impact on specific individuals, including Fertility, Euthanasia, Elderly Care, Sensory Perception, Pleasure Drugs, Prostitution, Marriage, Discrimination, Mental, Physical and Social Disabilities, Violence and Abuse, Obesity, Privacy, Private Property, Carrying Arms, and Access to Food, Water and Shelter.

Chapter 12: Economic Problems: explores ten interconnected global economic problems that are contributing to the serious inequities now facing humanity, including how we now manage The Market Place, Work, Job Sharing, Corporations, Cooperatives, Currency, Interest, Tax Avoidance and Money Laundering, Limited Liability and Bankruptcy.

Chapter 13: Equity Problems: Investigates twelve problems interfering with the development of peace on this planet including our forms of Government, Red Tape, Planning, Taking, Taxes, Language, Censorship, Armed Forces, Pacifism, Lawyers vs. Experts, Punishment and Justice.

Chapter 14: Community Problems: examines six basic global problems that can unintentionally but seriously affect social harmony, including the Media (social media and biased or fake news), Public Health Care, Public Education, Religious Persecution, Cultural Preservation and Social Support Systems for the unemployed, elderly and infirm.

Chapter 15: Environmental Problems: discusses twelve interrelated environmental problems that we need to address if humankind is to have a long term future on this planet, including Resource Sustainability, Climate Change, Natural Hazards, Movement, Transportation Networks, Nodal Growth, Effects Based Development, Rural Land Use, Land Banking, Energy Use, Pollution and Recycling, and Hazardous Substances.

Part C: Putting the Puzzle Together

Chapter 16: The Principles and Structures of a Consensus Based Democracy: describes the 5 basic principles of a consensus based democratic government. It defines several key terms like "site" and "public path" and it sets out a self-checking, self correcting set of "Structural Details" to ensure good governance in addition to the standard executive, legislative and judicial functions found in our current democracies.

Chapter 17: The Financial Implications: discusses several possible modifications to institutional finance that could be made to a new government which uses consensus decision-making to improve democratic outcomes. These include eliminating easily evaded income and business taxes and replacing them with a fixed "Resource Use Tax" and a "Goods and Services Tax", introducing the

"Living Wage" in exchange for guaranteed, mutually agreed work in the public sector and providing social, medical and old age support services to all, primarily through a two tiered monetary system.

Chapter 18: Sociocracy and Other Similar Paradigm: describes how a number of governments, businesses, schools and other organizations have already been established using many of the ideas set out in this book. It describes the history of Sociocracy in the Netherlands, and its use particularly in business. It also discusses its parallels with Jose Arizmendiarrietta's work in Mondragon, Spain and the extensive work of Edwin John in helping to set up thousands of similar governing groups in India.

Part D: The Planetary "Fix" (This booklet)

Chapter 19: A Way Out of This Mess: describes how an updated version of democracy using a "structured" version of consensus decision-making could be introduced over time to any sized group of people, anywhere, in just 5 steps. The first step would involve people trying out consensus decision making in their own club meetings, family outings and other non-threatening decision-making situations just to see how much less divisive it is. The last step would be voluntarily adopting the "Consocratice Plan" as an upgrade or amendment to an existing government's constitution or a corporation's management procedures.

Chapter 20: The Consocratic Plan: is a complete set of Goals, Principles, Rights, Responsibilities and Rules, that any sized group of people could voluntarily adopt over time to progressively and peacefully update local, regional and national democratic governments (and other institutions and businesses) without breaking any existing civil laws and procedures, and without having to resort to violence, terrorism or war.

About the Author:
Ted Wells

Ted was born and raised near Boston, Massachusetts and educated as an Architect and Urban Designer in Oregon and Colorado. After completing his degree in the sixties, he chose to join the Peace Corps in Ethiopia rather than the war in Vietnam.

For three years he planned new towns in very remote parts of the Rift Valley while his wife, Helen, treated sick people and cattle there. They then spent a year travelling the back roads of Europe in a VW van exploring their new towns to see what he should have done in Africa. Eventually they returned to the United States where he worked for 5 years as a planner for a small city in Colorado.

In the mid-1970s, he and his wife became disillusioned with American politics so they moved their young family to New Zealand in search of an alternative approach to peace, social justice and the environment. They found a comfortable home and welcoming community by the Tasman Sea and decided to stay.

As a dual US-New Zealand citizen, his professional planning career has taken him around the globe many times writing, studying and/or designing plans for governments, NGOs and businesses across the USA, Canada, the Caribbean, Great Britain, Europe, North Africa, China, Korea, Japan, Malaysia and the South pacific.

He has written plans for several US communities, the World Bank, the Japanese Aid Agency, a Gold Mine, the Sultan of Brunei, the Emperor of Ethiopia (just before he was killed) and for dozens of city, regional and national governments around the Pacific Rim including New Zealand, Australia, Samoa and Papua New Guinea. He has also been on the New Zealand Planning Institute's Governing Board of Directors, written articles for several journals and helped win for BECA Consultants, his employer for much of this time, several professional planning awards.

Both his books, "Power, Chaos or Consensus?" and "The Old Man in the Bag" are about some of his professional and personal travels and the ideas he has come across working on the edge of political decision-making in various parts of the world, which have given him hope there could be a better future for us.

It was in Ethiopia where Ted first learned that even selfless good intentions don't always leave those being "helped" with smiles on their faces; that life decisions are rarely ever black and white even though most of our public institutions currently force us to solve problems by first polarizing their possible solutions.

However, it was not until he spent two years in Samoa four decades later that he finally understood just how there might be another way through the current global mess we now find ourselves in. It was there helping local communities prepare coastal management plans against sea level rise due to global warming that he realised their centuries old consensus decision-making methods held the solution.